Never the Same

Never the Same

Coming to Terms
with the Death of a Parent

Donna
Schuurman

St. Martin's Press ⚏ New York

www.stmartins.com

Library of Congress Cataloging-in-Publication Data

Schuurman, Donna.
   Never the same : coming to terms with the death of a parent / Donna
Schuurman.—1st. ed.
      p. cm.
  ISBN 0-312-26210-8 (hc)
  ISBN 0-312-33095-2 (pbk)
  EAN 978-0312-33095-8
  1. Bereavement in children. 2. Parents—Death—Psychological aspects.
3. Bereavement—Psychological aspects. I. Title.

BF723.G75 S35   2003
155.9'37'0854—dc21   2002014406

D10 9 8 7 6 5 4 3 2

To all of the courageous children and adults
at The Dougy Center
for Grieving Children & Families
in Portland, Oregon

Contents

Acknowledgments

Thanks to my parents, Clare R. May and Charles W. May, who brought me into this world and gave me the best tools they could to negotiate in it. I only wish my father had lived long enough to be able to read this.

I'd also like to thank the friends, family, therapists, and colleagues who made it possible for me to understand what I've shared in this book. You truly are my teachers. Among those I'd like to thank by name: Anne Avery, David and Julia Bennett, Don Bennett, Gwyneth Gamble Booth, Kellie Campbell, Ann and Brian Carlton, Sharrin Chandler, Beverly Chappell, Lynne Ann DeSpelder, Linda Fritz, Linda Goldman, Stephen Guntli, LaVone Hazell, Mary Hochstetler, Cheryl Hollatz-Wisely, Michael Hubbard, Marylyn John, Earl Laman, Susan Leo, Betty May, Bradley William May, Stephen Charles May, Christine Phyllis McClave, Lexi Parrott, Barbara Paul, Julie Rushton, Richard and Ann Schuurman, Richard J. Schuurman, Joan Schweizer-Hoff, Izetta Smith, Don Spencer, Albert Lee Strickland, Cole Struhar, Anne Sweet, Diane Syrcle, Michele Weiner-Davis, Cynthia White, and Fran White.

Special thanks to my editor, Julia Pastore, who was a breeze to work with.

Introduction

If one or both of your parents died before you were eighteen years old, this book will help you and those who love you to understand you better. If there's one belief I hold as fact about the impact of your parent's death on you, it's this: You never "get over it." You are never the same. Your life is not the same as it would have been had your father or mother lived. Influenced for better or for worse by your parent, you would have taken different paths than you have.

But wait, you say. I've turned out okay. I'm not an axe murderer or a serial rapist. I've never embezzled money,

and I'm a decent _____ [fill in the blank: person, spouse, parent, friend, lover].

And yet, over the years, you sometimes wonder how the course of your life might have been different, how *you* might have been different, if your parent had not died.

In the years since your parent died, have you ever:

- felt a sense of being different?
- thought no one could possibly understand what you went through?
- felt you aren't sure YOU understand what you went through and how it affected you?
- had a sense that you haven't fully dealt with the impact your parent's death had on you and your family?
- wanted to connect the puzzle pieces of your life, increase your self-understanding, and grow?

Whether you're twenty-five, forty-five, or sixty-five, if you had a parent die when you were a child or teenager, the adults in your life probably had no idea what to say to you about this traumatic event in your life. The veil of secrecy most children experience following a parent's death is not a plot. Most adults simply don't know how to treat children when death strikes.

It wasn't until Elisabeth Kubler-Ross began her groundbreaking efforts in the late 1960s to bring death out of the closet that the taboo was broached, if not broken. And it wasn't until the mid-1980s before anyone in the

United States, including experts in the field of death and dying, began to seriously talk about children and how they were impacted by death. Progress has been made over the last couple of decades, but there's still a long way to go.

My interest in writing this book initially grew out of my work as the executive director of The Dougy Center, The National Center for Grieving Children & Families in Portland, Oregon. The center was the first group peer-support program in the United States for children, teens, and their parent or adult caregivers who've experienced the death of a family member. Since The Dougy Center's founding in 1982, more than twelve thousand children and teens have participated in support groups after the death of a parent, brother, or sister.

The groups meet every other week for an hour and a half, and the kids participate based on their age, who died, and how. The majority of them had a parent die, and father's deaths are represented more frequently than mother's. That's partially a result of demographics—more men than women die during the age ranges represented—and partially our society's acceptance of women seeking help more than men seeking help. Children as young as three attend the groups for "Littles" up through age five. Pre- and early adolescents can attend groups for six to twelve year olds or ten to fourteen year olds, and teens from thirteen to nineteen meet together. Some groups deal specifically with a death by suicide, by homicide, through a sudden death, or after a lengthy illness. Others are mixed losses. While the kids' groups meet, there's also a group for their surviving parent or adult caregiver. Usually these groups meet separately, but several times a year the kids and parents have opportunities to participate in activities together and to look at where they are in their healing process. Some children or teens attend The Dougy Center with a foster care worker or other adult who has legal custody or permission from their legal custodian, because their parent or parents are out of the picture or incapacitated. Of course, not all of the families we see were happy or high functioning prior to the death they've experienced. They represent a range of socioeconomic and educational levels but share the common denominator of a death.

There is no fee for the services of The Dougy Center, and it receives no government support or insurance reimbursements; the center exists through the contributions of thousands of individuals, businesses and foundations.

In response to requests, The Dougy Center began a training program and other resources to assist other communities in developing services for children and teens following loss through death. Over 130 programs have developed throughout the United States and into Canada, Australia, Japan, Germany, and beyond. For a listing of services and resources, see the center's Web site at www.dougy.org.

A unique aspect of the center's program, and certainly

counter to the current short-term emphasis of managed care, is that families attend for as long as they feel they need to. Some participate for six months; others as long as three years or more. It is the center's philosophy that because each person's grief experience is vastly different, we cannot impose a certain or expected time frame for their length of participation. Grief, we know, is not a six-week program.

The need for such a place as The Dougy Center is unfortunate. It exists only because our society fails to provide a safe place for children, teens, and adults to grieve and to heal following a death. As adults, we're typically permitted three days of bereavement leave, and often people avoid us when we return to work. For kids, the experience of returning to school, of facing friends and feeling different, and returning to a forever changed world can be overwhelming, especially when the adults around them don't know what to say or how to help.

When The Dougy Center's founder, former nurse Beverly Chappell, first envisioned a safe place for grieving families to share their feelings and experiences with one another, she was met with resistance from the medical and mental health communities. "We don't want anyone messing with our patients' heads," explained a prominent pediatrician. Another professional summed up a commonly held belief: "Kids are resilient; they'll get over it." While I believe we all have the inborn capacity to heal, and many kids show tremendous resilience, I don't believe that any child "gets over" the death of a parent. You get through it (or you don't), you readjust, go on, stumble around, find ways to cope, but you don't *get over* it. You are forever changed by this loss.

Although many children display an astounding ability to rebound from difficult situations, this doesn't occur in a vacuum. Time does not heal all wounds, despite the popularity of the phrase. Wounds heal through attending to the necessary conditions of healing: paying attention to the wound, keeping it clean and free from dirt and infection, having it bandaged at times, and at others exposed to the air. Without the proper care and attention, wounds fester, get infected, remain painful, and leave scars. I believe this is as true for emotional wounds as it is for physical ones.

The idea that children's natural resiliency will enable them to bounce back, overcome the odds, and "get over" traumatizing events has some threads of truth. But more recent research, which we'll examine later in this book, reveals the fallacy of this folklore when applied to all children. The children who bounce back, who overcome potentially destructive circumstances, whose resiliency wins out, share some common traits and circumstances. So do nonresilient children.

Another reason I became interested in writing this book is that over the years I've spoken with hundreds of adults who've lost a parent as a child through cancer, car wrecks, suicide, accidents, or murder. We've met on airplanes in the course of conversations about work, at parties, through my talks, and at The Dougy Center. More than half of our adult volunteers find themselves drawn to volunteer because they wish there had been a place like The Dougy Center for them when their own parent died when they were a child. When a seventeen-minute segment on The Dougy Center aired on ABC's *20/20* in 1992, our six-person staff was overwhelmed with over two thousand phone calls the following week, and more than eight hundred letters from around the country. Many of the letters were from adults who'd had a parent die ten, twenty, or thirty years prior. They universally expressed how much they wished that they'd had a place like The Dougy Center to go to when their parent died. And they poured out, sometimes in ten or twenty handwritten pages, what has become of their family since that pivotal event.

As I listened to adults who were bereaved as children talk about their experiences, themes began to emerge. The ways in which they talked about what happened, and how they felt, fell into some overlapping patterns. But this presented me with a formidable challenge: I believe every person's story is unique, yet I'm writing about commonalities. No one in the world has experienced the specific circumstances of your parent's death, not even your siblings. Your age, gender, maturity level, relationship with your deceased and surviving parent, friends, and other support systems all contribute to your particular story.

Since the death, you've built and lost relationships, gained and lost memories, and lived your life deeply affected by your parent's death and the meaning it had for you. That meaning, and your actions, may be ones you've thought about, discussed in therapy or with friends and family, and understand. It may also include areas you're not clear about, have repressed, or simply have never considered. We all have areas of ourselves we don't allow into our consciousness, in part because we tend to push into our unconscious that which is too painful, or too confusing, or both. It's impossible to completely and fully know ourselves—as Oscar Wilde pointed out, "Only the shallow know themselves." But the degree to which we become conscious of how life events have influenced us is the degree to which we will take responsibility and exercise choice around our own lives.

Although I've interviewed for this book many adults who were bereaved as children, observed thousands of grieving children and teens since my work with them began in 1986, read extensively in both popular and scholarly journals and books, and received a doctorate in counseling, I have not spoken directly with you. Parts of what is discussed here will pertain to you, and other parts won't. Please filter my words and apply them as you see fit. You are the best judge of what you need.

Maybe you did not personally have a parent die, but you're in a relationship with someone who did. As I've discussed the topic of this book with people in my travels and trainings, many have expressed how they believe their husband, wife, partner, or friend has been affected by the early death of their parent. This book will help you better understand, and support, your spouse, partner, or friend. If you're reading this for a loved one, you can serve an important role in their journey. If you invite them to share with you, you may be the first person who has ever asked! You may be the first person they have ever chosen to share with about the death of their parent. Know that listening without judgment will be the greatest gift you can offer.

If you're reading this for yourself, in the pages that follow you will:

- look at the common experiences of children and teens who've had a parent die, and gain new insight into your experience;
- explore how your parent's death impacted your development and how it continues to affect you in your life now;
- see what you needed in order to grieve healthfully— and what consequences occur when those conditions are not met;
- explore, understand, and reconcile how your life has been and continues to be influenced by your parent's death; and
- reconnect the "missing pieces" so you can live an

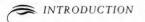

even more healthy, productive, satisfying, and peaceful life.

The following quiz will give you a better sense of your own experience and its subsequent effect upon your life.

WHAT'S TRUE FOR ME?
An Assessment of My Experience After My Parent's Death

As a quick exercise to see how your experience compares to that of others who had a parent die in childhood or adolescence, check off any of the following statements that are true for you:

___ When my parent died, no one included me in discussions or fully explained everything that had happened.

___ For a long time after my parent's death, I felt alone and isolated.

___ My family, and other adults, didn't talk together much about my deceased parent in the months following his or her death.

___ My family members still don't talk about it much.

___ Since the time my parent died, I've always felt different.

_____ No one gave me all the facts and information. In fact, I still have unanswered questions, and there are many things I don't know.

_____ I wasn't given a choice about attending the memorial service, funeral home, or cemetery.

_____ As far as the "disposition of the body," I had no opportunity to say how I felt about burial versus cremation, where my parent would be buried, the type of service, or participation in the service.

_____ I felt like I had to be strong for everyone else.

_____ It was hard going back to school.

_____ I had many difficult times around holidays and the anniversary of my parent's death.

_____ I still have difficulties with holidays, and/or the anniversary time of my parent's death.

_____ I didn't talk about it much to anyone back then.

_____ I haven't really talked all that much to others as an adult about how my parent's death impacted me.

_____ I wanted to "protect" my surviving parent, so I didn't talk about it with him or her.

_____ As a kid, or sometimes as an adult, I thought I had something to do with my parent's death.

____ I didn't really know many, if any, other kids who'd had a parent die.

____ I remember blaming myself for something I did or failed to do that contributed to my parent's death.

____ I remember having some experiences or feelings that made me wonder if I was going crazy or if something was wrong with me.

____ There are parts of what happened when my parent died that remain a blur.

____ For a long time I put it out of my mind and didn't think about it.

____ We didn't do much as a family around the anniversary date of my parent's death.

____ I sometimes wonder how things would have been different if my parent hadn't died.

____ At some point in my adult life, I realized I had been greatly affected by my parent's death.

____ I suspect that in some ways my adult relationships have been influenced by how I responded to my parent's death, but I'm not sure what they are.

SCORING

Now, count how many statements you have checked:

——

Here's what your responses indicate:

0–5 statements:

You should have written this book or should be writing your own! Seriously. If none of the twenty-five statements above are true for you, your experience is extremely rare. The adults around you apparently handled the aftermath of your parent's death in a supportive way, and you have completed some significant work in your adult psychological life. Or . . . is it possible you're in denial? Either way, I encourage you to read this book, even if it's just to emphasize how many things went right for you.

6–10 statements:

There was a great deal of support for you when your parent died, and you feel fairly resolved about how it has affected you. You're in the minority here, but there still may be some avenues left for you to explore.

11–15 statements:

You're confused about the impact your parent's death had on you as a child, and what work you have

left to do. There are still some important roads you have not walked along. Your sense of self, and your relationships, can be strengthened if you apply what's written here.

16–20 statements:

You will benefit tremendously from reading this book, hearing about the experiences of others, and exploring what your parent's death means for you now. You likely have had difficulty with intimacy in your relationships and have felt like something is disconnected inside of you.

21–25 statements:

Stop whatever you have planned for the next several days, carve out some time alone, and read this book. It could help you make some significant positive changes in your life. The quality of all of your relationships is related to your relationship with yourself, and there are parts—important parts—you have not explored.

However many of these statements are true for you, take heart in the belief that you're reading this book at this time in your life because you're ready to do so. Experiencing your parent's death changed the course of your life in some good ways and in some ways that have not served you well.

Your parent's death forced a premature maturity on you compared to your peers. As a result, you have a deeper inner knowledge about what is important in life and how quickly people who matter can be taken away from us.

The death of your parent did not in and of itself destine you for relationship issues, bouts of depression, anxiety, guilt, or fear. But if you were not able to make sense as a child or teen of what was happening around and inside of you, you have areas of unconsciousness about yourself that control you without your awareness. It's not only the death, but the sense you made of it, that matters now.

Never the Same

CHAPTER ONE

Feelings:
Forget the Stages

*Learn your theories well, but lay them aside
when you touch the reality of the living soul.*

—Carl Jung

If you pick up a book about grief or loss, chances are that
it will include a section about stages, phases, or tasks of
grieving. These may or may not fit your experience, but
they're attempts by professionals to make sense of—to find
patterns in—what happens to people when a death occurs.
Theories are, as the developmental psychologist Erik Erikson said, "a jab at the unknown."

Part of the reason why clinicians and educators want to
build theories and models is to help us assess ourselves
against some standard. To help us know if our reactions are
"normal," and therefore if we're okay. When we're talking

about kids grieving a death, this benchmark of normal is important because one of the most common concerns of grieving kids is the fear of being different. Think about it. When your parent died, didn't you automatically feel different?

You *were* different. Through no fault of your own, you were suddenly thrown into a new and frightening existence. You had to deal, not only with your own feelings of loss and uncertainty, but also with the reality that the people around you—your friends, family members, neighbors—saw you as different. They didn't know how to relate to you. You wanted everyone to treat you like they always had, but that was hard for people to do. They were afraid they'd make you feel worse if they talked about what happened. Your family members were dealing with their own grief and hardly had enough energy left over to consider yours, though they wanted to. You just wanted everything to return to normal.

But what is normal? This is where theories can be of some help. Theories are attempts to help us understand where we are compared to the rest of the population coping with our experience. Theories may help us know when additional help from a support group or professional counseling is beneficial. But theories may also be overapplied. They are, by nature, a removed process, a representation. The word itself derives from the Greek *theoros* meaning "spectator." So theory is a spectator sport, so to speak. You

2

know as a spectator at a sporting event, for example, you may cheer, curse, and scream; but you're not in the throes of the action on the field or court. You can describe and interpret what's happening (theorize), but the player's experience may stray from the bounds of your expectations and vary from your interpretation. Theories shouldn't be viewed as prescriptive boundaries we should try to fit ourselves into. They are simply attempts to try to make sense of common experiences and processes.

So let's take a quick look at three common theories about grieving, which take a "jab at the unknown."

Three Common Ways to Look at Grieving

Theories about grieving fall mostly into one of three kinds: stages, phases, or tasks. **Stages** have fallen out of favor, mostly because people latched on to them as if there were some orderly one-two-three way to grieve, and then be done with it. Perhaps the best known, least understood, and most misused theory about grieving is Elisabeth Kubler-Ross's pioneering model from her 1969 book, *On Death and Dying*.[1] The model includes five stages of grieving: numbness, denial, anger, blame, and acceptance. But the model has frequently been misapplied from her original intention. First, the steps evolved from her attempt to make sense of the process of people who were dying, not something applied to those grieving a death. Second, she did not intend, even then, to prescribe that the stages were sequential, orderly, and mandatory. Over the years, I've had many calls from people who've said things like: "It's been a year since my mother died, and everyone told me I'd feel better in a year . . . but I don't. Is something wrong with me?" or "I feel very sad about my father's death, and cry a lot, but I haven't felt angry. People are telling me that until I get angry, I'm not really dealing with it. What should I do?"

One of the consequences of the stages theories of grief is that people may be led to believe that they're grieving "incorrectly," that there's some prescribed way to do it. Forget the stages. Each person's experience is unique. When your father or mother died, you found your own individual way of coping. You didn't follow anyone's stages.

Phase theories are fairly similar to stage theories. One of the initial pioneers in the area of grieving was J. Bowlby and his work on attachment and loss.[2] He was one of the first professionals to talk about grief and mourning as they affect how we relate to others. The first of four phases he proposed was a period of numbing, where you experience a kind of protective disbelief about the death. It's like a psychological parallel of the body's tendency to go into shock following a traumatic physical injury as a way of protecting yourself from pain. The numbness is followed

4

by yearning and searching, where you feel intense longing, deep distress, and anger: *I miss my dad. I feel terrible! Why did this have to happen to me?* The third phase, disorganization, involves your search for the "how" and "why" of the death. Finally, there is reorganization, when you try to re-define yourself in relationship to the loss and to your deceased parent, both intellectually and emotionally.

As with stage models, phase theories provide helpful attempts for professionals to build models of grieving, but the model is not "the thing itself." You may or may not have felt numb, deep distress and anger, disorganization, or confusion, when your parent died. (Some kids actually report feeling relieved.) Most likely whatever you felt didn't happen in an organized way. More likely, some things got better, and some things got worse.

J. William Worden, a research psychologist and clinician, rejected stage and phase models as passive, and developed a **four-task model** that he believed better addressed the active nature of grieving.[3] These tasks include accepting the reality of the loss, working through the pain of grief, adjusting to an environment in which the deceased is missing, and emotionally relocating the deceased and re-investing in other relationships.

I view Worden's task model as an attempt to assist clinicians, and ultimately grievers, to understand and actively participate in the process of healing after a death, rather than considering themselves passive victims. These tasks

5

may provide a helpful lens through which to view actions that may help in the healing process. On the other hand, they may be viewed as additional burdens and yet more work, more "shoals" in the already draining and difficult experience of grieving. For example, can you remember when you accepted the reality of your parent's death, if ever? Do you ever find yourself thinking perhaps it didn't happen, that he or she will call one day, will show up at your door, will write you a letter saying it's all a cruel mistake? How would acknowledging the fact of the death and accepting that it was okay differ? Is it wrong to wish it hadn't happened? Does "working through the pain of grief" place another layer of expectations on you? "Adjusting to the new environment" may take years, or a lifetime. And how have you—or have you?—maintained a connection with your deceased parent while at the same time reinvesting in other healthy relationships? This isn't something most people probably encouraged you to do. Rather, they more commonly urged you to "move on," to "put it behind you," and to "forget." Worden's model, as with other task models, has merit, but may also unwittingly place additional burdens on grievers to "get it right."

These common theories have been expanded upon by many experts in the field of death and dying, and are continually being refined and adjusted. But again, no theory is ever going to provide you with a magic bullet. It may be helpful to read about them, to know something about them, but don't try to fit yourself into anyone's mold. Your story is different from everyone else's in the world.

Getting Prepared to Look at How Your Parent's Death Has Affected You

Before we take a closer look at how your parent's death has affected your life, I'd like to ask you to consider doing something that sounds simple, but it isn't something most of us are accustomed to doing. If you make the commitment to do what I suggest, you will find yourself experiencing some radical positive changes in yourself and in your relationships.

As we begin to talk about feelings and relationships, you're going to find yourself alternately opening and closing your mind and your feelings. You'll open up when you read something that fits, confirms your experience, makes sense to you, or hooks onto a part of you. You'll close down when something feels too painful, embarrassing, or threatening. This is normal. We all do it. It's also automatic, or at least it seems that way. Over time, we build patterns of responding, and we tell ourselves, "This is how I am." It doesn't feel like we're choosing those patterns; it feels like they're choosing us. But we are actually choosing our thoughts, our feelings, and our actions all the time. They are efforts on our part to protect ourselves. But one of the

7

consequences of shutting down when we feel threatened is that we cut ourselves off from ourselves—we deaden ourselves. So what I'm asking you to do is treat yourself with the same kindness and compassion you would treat someone else through the following four actions.

Be Honest with Yourself

First, be honest, and allow yourself to look at and feel the hard stuff. It's there. Your avoidance of it does not make it disappear. You already know this. The reason we don't want to acknowledge painful issues is simple: it hurts, and we don't want to be in pain. There's nothing inherently wrong with that. If you place your hand on a hot stove burner, your automatic response is to pull it off (stop what is causing the pain) and then treat the burn (take steps toward healing). If you leave your hand on the burner, denying that it hurts, your denial does not change the fact that your hand is burning. If you take it off the burner but refuse to treat it, it will fester, possibly get infected, take longer to heal, and leave deeper scars. Yet we often leave our hand on the burner or refuse to treat our burnt palm when it comes to psychological pain. Take the radical risk of allowing yourself to be honest, even when it's painful.

Don't allow your usual patterns of avoidance to distract you from finishing this book. What are those patterns? Here are some common ones:

- I numb myself with alcohol.
- Alcohol is not my drug of choice—I use _____.
  (You might not want to fill in this blank in case you leave this book lying around.)
- I keep myself busy, often with tasks that don't really matter.
- I clean my house/office when I'm really avoiding something!
- I work, work, work.
- I get depressed and withdraw from my family and friends.
- I watch too much TV.
- I go shopping.
- I eat. And eat.
- I throw myself into compulsive exercise.
- I have a hobby that seems healthy but has actually developed into an obsession.
- Other: _____

It takes honesty to admit your patterns of avoidance, and it takes courage not to give in to them. So hang in there and be honest with yourself when you're tempted to run. I don't mean to suggest that all avoidance is necessarily bad. There are also times where you will need to put your thoughts or feelings on the back burner, and you can choose to postpone or take breaks from looking at this material. Just know that whatever you're avoiding will be there, waiting for you.

Build Awareness of How You Avoid

Knowing your patterns of avoidance leads right into the second action for your consideration as you explore the affects of your parent's death, and that is building awareness. You already have some awareness, or at least curiosity, about how your parent's death affects you, or you wouldn't be reading this book. But some parts of it may strike too close to home and may bring up painful memories or feelings. That's when you'll find yourself wanting to engage in your avoidance behaviors. When you feel yourself wanting to engage in your avoidance patterns, recognize that behavior. Allow yourself to be aware: Oh, I want a drink. Another pint of ice cream. I want to get out of this house. I need to work late tonight. Just five more pairs of shoes, and I'll feel better. Once you notice, you can make a decision about whether or not to continue the pattern. For example, I've realized that when I want to avoid something, I develop a strong desire to sleep. When I have a pressing deadline, or feel pressured by something, I can sleep for twelve hours. So when I find myself wanting to sleep irregular hours, I ask myself whether I might be avoiding something. On the other hand, I may be needing extra sleep, or I may be engaged in healthy avoidance by permitting my conscious mind to take a break. If I'm aware and notice my behavior, I can make choices about it. Avoidance energy actually saps a lot of our strength from us, and if these patterns are left unacknowledged, they may leave us feeling chronically tired and unmotivated.

Suspend the Judge

This may be your hardest action to take because, for most of us, our self-critic is a fully developed judge, jury, and executioner. Your third task is to suspend your self-judgment. It's a natural reactive human phenomenon to judge ourselves and others around us. We do it all the time. *I like those shoes. That was a stupid remark. I should have been nicer. What the heck is his problem?* But one of the reasons we keep our feelings stuffed inside us, and therefore experience self-alienation and the uncomfortable sense that all is not well (which we quickly squelch with our avoidance behaviors), is that we don't want to feel pain. When we reflect on painful experiences, relationships, or actions, it hurts. It hurts more because of *what we tell ourselves* about those experiences, relationships, and actions. *I was a fool. I should have known better. He was a jerk. I'm smarter than that.* It's an act of self-protection to place blame on ourselves, on someone else, or both, when relationships don't work out as we'd like them to.

Imagine that someone you love seeks your counsel and

comfort. Imagine that she comes to you describing a painful loss, the ending of a relationship. Because you love her, you want to encourage her, but you don't want to lie just to make her feel better. (Okay, you're tempted to lie to help her feel better, but you recognize that's not really loving.) Would you say to her, "You were a fool. You should have known better! You're smarter than that. What in the world were you thinking?" And yet we tell *ourselves* messages like this all the time. Begin to see how many times your internal critic gives you messages that are not loving. When our internal critic tells us we're stupid, rude, thoughtless, foolish, and whatever other slurs we slap on ourselves, no wonder we want to run away!

What if . . . you could notice yourself with compassion, without judgment? I'm not suggesting you dismiss morality, or that there aren't helpful and hurtful actions and ways of being. But sometimes our quickness to judge ourselves harshly prevents us from making changes that could actually help us live healthier, happier, and more productive lives. Although it doesn't always appear that way, our feelings, our thoughts, and our actions are purposeful. We choose them. What we tell ourselves about an event colors the corresponding feeling. Sometimes it seems as if our feelings are mysterious bursts of energy that strike randomly and without reason. But in actuality, we create our feelings by what we tell ourselves about what happens.

Here's a simple illustration. About an hour ago, I was

happily typing along and the screen on my computer froze. I've had this happen a few times and have lost paragraphs or pages as a result, an extremely frustrating experience. The only recourse was to push the off button, reboot, and try to reconstruct whatever was lost. As I sat waiting for the computer to restart, my initial response was frankly, well, not printable here. I told myself a terrible thing had happened, that I'd lost not only my valuable words, but my thought process and time as well. I wanted to throw the computer through the window. I almost worked myself into enough of a frenzy that I could've used it as a great excuse to stop writing and do something else. Like sleep. Like eat a pint of Starbucks's Java Chip ice cream. So my thought *(this is terrible)* was followed by emotions (anger, frustration) that led to possible actions (avoidance under the guise of self-reward).

Then I realized I was creating this whole scenario, and that I had a choice about how I wanted to respond. I decided not to let this minor setback stop me from writing, and to reframe it as a needed break, a fluke of my computer, and an opportunity to act on my commitment to continue writing. So I changed my thought *(this is no big deal; at worst, it's a temporary setback),* which was followed by emotions (pride, excitement) that led to actions (continuing writing).

I also could have told myself I shouldn't feel whatever I felt, and the judge part could have sabotaged my writing time. Instead, I noted that at first I felt angry and frustrated. Rather than allow those feelings, or my judgment of those feelings, to control my emotions and actions, I decided to try out another script. But it's hard to not allow our emotions to carry us away or our judgments of ourselves to lead us off track. See if you can suspend your self-judgment, at least with regard to how you've responded to your parent's death. Whatever you have done, it has been an attempt to regain your equilibrium.

Ask for Support

Perhaps *this* will be your most difficult step. Many of us have difficulty admitting that we can't do everything on our own, that we could use support or assistance, especially when we're having troubling feelings or thoughts. We don't want to burden others; don't want them to think we're weak. (We don't want to think it ourselves!)

But this is not a journey you should or need to embark on alone. If you checked off many boxes in the self-assessment exercise, you've already experienced years of isolation and lack of support around your parent's death. Take the risk to allow those who care about you to support you. Anyone who truly loves and cares about you will welcome the opportunity to be present with you. You may want to read this book with someone, or share the results of the quiz in the beginning.

A word of caution: Be selective in who you ask to accompany you on this journey, and make sure it's someone who is interested in your story and in supporting you. Many of us have been taught that the best way to deal with pain is to ignore it or push it away. Some people believe it's not helpful to "dredge up" the past. Some people are unable to provide support because of their own unexplored grief issues. But among your circle of family members, friends, and colleagues try to identify at least one person you can share your journey with. You've already spent much of your life carrying the impact of your parent's death alone. Asking for and receiving support will help you better process how your parent's death affected, and continues to affect, you.

So are you willing to take these four actions as you read on?

1. Be honest with yourself about your feelings and your usual patterns of avoidance.
2. Be aware of when you want to avoid your feelings.
3. Suspend your critical self-judge.
4. Enlist the support of at least one person who cares about you.

Now, with honesty, awareness, self-acceptance, and support, let's take a look at what kind of grieving kid you were.

My Notes

Was I a Normal Grieving Kid?

In the years after your parent's death, did you feel a sense of being different? If so, you're not alone. One of the most common concerns I've heard bereaved children and adolescents express revolves around the answer to a simple question: *Am I normal?* They ask it in direct and indirect ways. Here are a few examples:

Fourteen-year-old Jason, whose father died, shared that "I felt like a freak when I went back to school, like everyone was staring at me. Like I had a big 'D' for 'dead' engraved on my forehead or something. Everybody was acting weird around me, and I just wanted to be who I always was, to fit in. But I felt totally different from everyone else."

Nine-year-old DeShe'a was afraid she was "going crazy" when she experienced some common symptoms of grieving after her mother's death. "I would be in my room and everything was fine, and then for no reason I would start shaking and couldn't stop. Or I'd see someone and think it was my mom, and I'd run up to her and then find out it wasn't her. I felt really stupid."

Even young children sense that they are different from other kids after a parent dies. During one of The Dougy Center's "Littles" groups for three to five year olds, Luke got a splinter in his finger while climbing on the playhouse outside. He went inside with an adult facilitator for a Band-Aid, trailed by his buddy, Mario. Both of these preschoolers' fathers had died in car accidents. As Luke's finger was washed and the Band-Aid applied, Mario said that he too had a "boo-boo" and needed a Band-Aid. When the facilitator asked him where his boo-boo was, he replied, "It's invis'ble. All of us kids at The Dougy Center have invis'ble boo-boos, 'cause we all had someone die." He knew, even at four, that he was different from other kids.

You may still wonder whether your experiences as a child after your parent's death were common or normal, especially if you didn't know other kids who had had a parent die. But the issue of what's normal begs another question—

who decides what is normal? When applied to grief, the answers can get fuzzy because what may be normal may feel or look "crazy" to the griever or to observers. There's a vast literature in *thanatology*—the study of death—around the differences between "normal" and "pathological" grief. Yet, like pornography, it's easier to recognize when you see it than it is to define it. One scholarly description of *pathological grief* is "where grief for a particular individual, in a particular culture, appears to deviate from the expected course in such a way that it is associated with excessive or prolonged psychological or physical morbidity."[1] Excessive or prolonged morbidity refers to an increased rate or intensity of mental or physical illness. But the explanation also implies that cultural norms set the standard from which the griever must "deviate" in order to be classified as suffering from pathological grief. The issues raised here are not small ones: Who determines what your "expected course" should look like, given who you are and the culture you grew up in? How do we address the reality that for many years even many "experts," including physicians, psychologists, and psychiatrists, had little training in, or understanding of, how children grieve? If our cultural norm is that men shouldn't cry, does this mean a man who cries is expressing pathological grief?

The term *pathology* has many variations, including complicated, absent, abnormal, distorted, morbid, maladaptive, delayed, chronic, atypical, intensified, masked, prolonged, unresolved, neurotic, dysfunctional, and inhibited. Still, against what standard, and what "expected course" do we measure *normal* behavior? Assessing whether your experience was typical, and whether your feelings and responses were normal, is not simple. Yet this question continues to haunt many bereaved children into adulthood as they struggle with continuing feelings of being different from others.

Although many research studies have looked at the effect of parental bereavement, comparatively few have used scientifically sound methods. Before we look at what some solid studies have shown on this topic, take a few minutes to check off which of the following statements you believe represent your experience as a child or teenager in the years after your parent's death:

1. _____ I felt depressed and withdrawn.
2. _____ I was very social and enjoyed being with others.
3. _____ I had more health problems or accidents.
4. _____ I rarely got sick, had stomachaches, sleeping problems, or injuries.
5. _____ I didn't do as well in school as I could have.
6. _____ I exceeded my expectations for success in school.
7. _____ I felt anxious and fearful.
8. _____ I felt happier and more carefree than kids around me.

9. _____ I didn't really feel good about myself.

10. _____ I felt as competent as anyone else.

11. _____ I felt like the world was random and out of my control.

12. _____ I felt like I had control over my own destiny.

13. _____ I didn't feel very optimistic about my future.

14. _____ I felt like I could accomplish anything I set my mind to.

We will look at what your responses mean and how they compare to what studies have shown, but let me say something about what research does and what it doesn't do. Even studies with scientifically solid methods and instruments don't *prove* things. They indicate trends; they provide evidence for outcomes; they show possible increased likelihood that if you do X, you are more at risk for Y than someone who doesn't do X. Smoking cigarettes is a good example. Although the surgeon general has "determined" that smoking causes cancer, not everyone who smokes will get cancer. And not everyone who gets cancer smokes. There is, in other words, scientific evidence for an association between smoking and cancer. Your risk for getting cancer increases if you smoke, but no one can say with absolute certainty that if you smoke you *will* get cancer.

So it's important to note that when you look at the results of any kind of research, its conclusions indicate trends, show probabilities, and provide fuel for theories.

They don't *prove* or *predict* what might happen in any one individual's situation. Another caveat about conclusions of research studies: You can find a study to support anything you believe to be true. Without knowing how the study was conducted, it is impossible to weigh how credible the conclusions really are. Among thousands of studies of bereaved children, very few provide findings that can be generalized to anyone other than the children studied. A full discussion of the limitations of these studies is beyond the scope of this book (and probably beyond your interest), but I've summarized twelve common ones in the appendix in case you're interested.

Now back to your response to the fourteen statements at the beginning of this chapter. We'll look at what they mean, but first, here's how to score your answers:

1. Count how many odd-numbered statements you checked. Your answer will be between 0 and 7:___
2. Count how many even-numbered statements you checked. Your answer will be between 0 and 7:___

The higher your score in number 1, that is, the more odd-numbered statements you checked, and the lower your score in number 2, that is, the fewer even-numbered statements you checked, the more representative your experience is, or the more "normal," compared to what sound studies have shown so far about the affects of parental bereavement on children.

If you checked off more even numbers than odd numbers (if your score in number 2 is higher than your score
in number 1) or if you *only* checked even-numbered sentences, you really bucked the trend. Later, we'll see what
contributed to your ability to do so. For now, let's look at
what light the methodologically sound studies shed on the
affects of parental bereavement in childhood. The studies
cited here are considered more methodologically sound
than others because for the most part they had a "control
group," that is, they compared the bereaved "sample" of
children or adolescents to a "sample" of similar children
who were not bereaved. They also used tests or measure-
ments with valid designs, administration, and interpretation.
Here are the seven findings that emerged from the studies
and how they relate to what you checked off in the statements earlier. Remember, these are studies of bereaved
children and don't address whether the same symptoms will
carry over into adulthood. We'll look at which do, which
don't, and why, in a later chapter.

The Significant Seven

Here are the seven significant differences that studies have
shown between bereaved children and their nonbereaved
counterparts.[2] The bereaved children show:

1. Higher levels of depression
2. An increase in health problems and accidents

23

3. Significantly poorer school performance
4. Significantly more anxiety and fear
5. Significantly lower levels of self-esteem
6. A significantly higher external locus of control
7. Significantly less optimism for success in later life

Let's look at your experience in each of these areas, and where you may have been most affected as a child after your parent's death.

Were You Depressed as a Child?

1. _____ I felt depressed and withdrawn.
2. _____ I was very social and enjoyed being with others.

Which of these sentences did you check? If you checked 1, your experience is more the norm for bereaved children than those who checked 2. Perhaps you're one of the few who checked both of these statements, indicating that on the outside you were social and liked being with others, while on the inside you felt depressed. Depression is the most common finding in the studies that have been conducted so far on childhood bereavement. It doesn't take a psychology degree to imagine the long-term affects of depression and how this mood in childhood *could* carry over into your adulthood. If you have experienced depression as an adult, you could be carrying an unnecessary legacy from your childhood.

24

Did You Have More Accidents or Health Problems Than Your Friends?

3. _____ I had more health problems or accidents.
4. _____ I rarely got sick, had stomachaches, sleeping problems, or injuries.

It's common for bereaved children at The Dougy Center to experience a vast range of physical symptoms including earaches, headaches, stomachaches, difficulty sleeping (or waking up), difficulty eating (or eating too much), as well as an increase in "accidents." Frequently no medical cause for the symptoms is found. We also see what seems to be (and which is supported by a study of bereaved children over time) a higher than average number of broken bones, cuts, and bruises. Sometimes we're told these kids are "acting out," and they're usually referred to us by frantic teachers or a frustrated parent. I see these kids as crying out for help and attention through their "acting out." Too often they're dismissed and ignored, which only leads to higher levels of attention-seeking behavior. Too often they're judged harshly as "wanting attention," as if wanting attention is a crime. All kids want and need attention. They'll continue to shout, often by their actions, until they're heard.

Although nine-year-old Stacy's behavior is at the extreme end of acting out, I think her experience illustrates dramatically what many of the bereaved children I've seen go through on a smaller scale. Stacy's father died by suicide, and she was teased by other children in her school. One day she came to group at The Dougy Center with a cast on her arm. I asked her what had happened, and she said she'd fallen off a swing set in the playground at school. Later in the group she told me, shyly and quietly, that she really hadn't fallen, but had let go on purpose. She explained why: "It hurts so bad that my dad is dead. No one cares. When I got to break my arm, the kids were nicer to me." Imagine what adolescence and adulthood could be for Stacy if she believes the only way to get attention is to be injured.

You may not have felt the need to act as dramatically to gain love and attention as Stacy did. But if you've had more than your share of illnesses or injuries, you may be playing out a need for attention and affection, even as an adult. We don't stop needing love and attention just because we age; we just learn to hide it better!

Did You Do as Well in School as You Think You Were Capable of Doing?

5. _____ I didn't do as well in school as I could have.
6. _____ I exceeded my expectations for success in school.

Several studies show that bereaved young people, as well as their parents, rate themselves as having poorer school performance than their classmates. Many kids, following a death, experience difficulty concentrating or find themselves disinterested in school, as well as other activities they once enjoyed. This makes a lot of sense to me. How interesting can academics be when you've just buried your father? How relevant can math feel when your mother just died? It's not uncommon for kid's grades to drop after they've had a death, nor is it uncommon for them to believe they're not keeping up with their peers.

How about you? Did you check 5? If so, you may have continued a pattern of underperformance into adulthood. (Or you may not be accurately assessing your performance. You may in fact be performing at a high standard but not acknowledging it to yourself. Or you may be setting your standards higher than they could ever be reached.) Or did you check 6? Although less common, some bereaved children throw themselves into their schoolwork as a way of "hypersucceeding." John, fifty-four, told me that after his father died when he was eleven, he knew if he was going to succeed in life, he'd have to do it on his own. So he applied himself to his schoolwork as he never had before, and he carried that work ethic into adulthood, with some positive, and some not as positive, consequences.

Were You Anxious and Fearful After Your Parent's Death?

7. _____ I felt anxious and fearful.

8. _____ I felt happier and more carefree than kids around me.

As might be expected, children and adolescents report feeling more anxiety and fear after the death of a parent than those who did not have a parent die. This normal and predictable response to an event that we view as outside of the order of things—our parents should be here for us and die of old age, or at least after we're grown up—is a logical reaction to an event that by its nature produces uncertainty. I have observed, though I can't scientifically prove it, that children who've had a death in the family seem to exhibit a wisdom beyond their chronological years. I've heard others describe them as "old souls." Perhaps the early knowledge of life's brevity, and that those around us can be taken away in an instant, forces a "hypermaturity," a kind of spiritual awareness that many of us don't confront until adulthood.

Your situation following your parent's death may have been filled with many reasons for you to be anxious and fearful. In addition to your parents' death, your life may have included many other losses and changes. Perhaps you moved, changed schools, or were separated from your siblings. You may have lived with adults who neglected or resented you. You may have been abandoned emotionally or literally, and left to parent yourself.

The larger and longer term issue is this: Have you carried that anxiety and fear into adulthood? If so, you are carrying a burden you don't have to bear forever. Later, we'll look at what to do about it.

If you checked 8, your experience was truly unusual! Rare is the child who reports less anxiety or fear after a parent's death, though I have run into a few in the last fifteen years. One, ten-year-old Joshua, had a physically abusive and alcoholic father. He told me he was glad his dad was dead, that life had become easier, and that he felt a lot less fear knowing his father's unpredictable anger wouldn't be directed at him or his mom. Kids like Joshua have taught me to be cautious using the words "loved one" to categorically describe the deceased. Not all deceased people would be described by family members as "loved," though I have yet to attend or hear about a funeral where someone stood up and said to the attendees, "Let's face it, folks. Aren't we all pretty relieved he's dead? Let's go celebrate!" I have yet to see a dead person described as a "hated one," yet there *are* children who hated their father or mother, or who had very conflicted feelings about them, particularly if there was abuse or mental illness. As you might imagine, feeling happy that a parent has died is generally not considered a "socially acceptable" response, and children with such reactions often feel doubly alone and different.

Do You View Yourself as Having High or Low Self-esteem After Your Parent's Death?

9. _____ I didn't really feel good about myself.
10. _____ I felt as competent as anyone else.

If you checked off 9, your response is a normal one for bereaved children. Several studies have shown significantly lower levels of self-esteem in bereaved children compared to their nonbereaved counterparts. While there's controversy about the role of self-esteem in success, and even how to "measure" it, most of us would agree that we tend to do better, feel better, and treat others better when we feel good about ourselves.

As thirteen-year-old Nathan expressed it, "When my dad died, I just felt like my whole world caved in, like I couldn't do as well without his help and support." Whether or not Nathan's father would have helped and provided the support he thought he needed are another matter. His reaction was based on what he told himself, not necessarily what may have played out had his father lived. This is an important distinction because self-esteem, like many self-assessments, has more to do with what we tell ourselves than what objective reality may show. (Some may even question whether there's such a thing as "objective reality.")

Many successful people have low self-esteem. Many people exhibit high self-esteem whose lives don't seem to substantiate the claim. Self-esteem is based more on the story we tell ourself about who we are than what others think, say, or believe. It doesn't always "feel" that way. But in truth, no one can *make* us feel one way or another. This is not to deny the affect others have on how we see ourselves. But as adults, we can choose to let the patterns of childhood continue, or we can recognize that we alone control how we feel about ourselves. If you have suffered from low self-esteem, a feeling that you're just not good enough, since your parent's death, it may be related to the stories you've told yourself, or the stories others have told you that you believed. It's not unusual for bereaved children to feel a lowered sense of self-esteem, but they are not fated to carry that into adulthood.

Did You Feel Like the World Was Out of Your Control, or That You Could Control What Happened to You?

11. _____ I felt like the world was random and out of my control.

12. _____ I felt like I had control over my own destiny.

If you checked 11, your experience is the more typical for bereaved children than nonbereaved children. Earlier, I expressed it as "bereaved children show a higher external locus of control." That's a fancy way of saying that bereaved children view the world as *happening to them* versus their having control of what happens. This makes complete sense, doesn't it? Children and adolescents are, by definition and developmental ability, egocentric, that is, they believe that the world revolves around them. (Most parents would agree that it does, at least for a while.) Our society generally supports and advocates for the ideal of a nuclear family, with a father, mother, and children who live together in the same home, even though nearly half of all children will experience their parent's divorce, and many children are now being raised in radically different family structures.

This is a good spot to say a few words about the effect of parental divorce and how it compares to parental death in childhood. Generally speaking, I don't care for viewing the impact of death or divorce as a competition: Divorce is harder, or death is harder. While I understand the importance of knowing how, when, and in what situations to intervene with children to prevent later difficulties in life, I don't believe enough quality research has been conducted to conclude that one over the other has a potentially more troubling outcome for children. In both situations, the child's beliefs about the security of his or her family have been shattered. In both cases, the children could not control the outcome of the events, even though they may believe they are somehow to blame. In both circumstances, the world feels random and out of his or her direct control.

In fact, many elements of the world *are* out of our control. The locus of control concept is an important one, however, because if you believe events around you generally happen randomly and beyond your control, you will behave very differently than someone who believes he or she *generally* has control over the events of life. We all know we can't control *everything;* but we tend to lean one way or the other—toward an external or internal locus of control. This difference, we will see later, plays a key role in how our lives as adults play out.

Did You Feel Optimistic or Pessimistic About Your Future?

13. _____ I didn't feel very optimistic about my future.
14. _____ I felt like I could accomplish anything I set my mind to.

If you checked statement 13, you're more the norm for a bereaved child than those who checked 14. When your parent died, there probably were some very realistic concerns about the future, especially if your family's financial stability was weakened. You may have wondered if you'd be able to go to college or fulfill other hopes and dreams. New obstacles probably did emerge in your path, so a dip in optimism about the future may have been justified.

Your family may have fallen apart completely after your parent died. You may have been raised by adults who didn't have your best interests in mind. You may have spent time in foster care, on the run, on the streets, in jail, or in situations that didn't provide much hope for the future. Whatever your unique situation and circumstances following your parent's death, it is not too late *now* to transform your experience with optimism and hope.

As in all of the seven findings discussed here, the key issue is not just what you experienced as a bereaved child, but what happened after that. Depression, health issues, a dip in school performance, increased anxiety, lower self-esteem, a more external locus of control, and a bit less optimism about the future have been shown to be common (therefore, "normal") reactions to the death of a parent in childhood. The next question to ask is this: As an adult, which of these symptoms have I continued to experience?:

- I have been depressed frequently in my adult life.
- I've had a fair amount of health problems or injuries.
- I don't believe I've lived up to my potential.
- I have a lot of fear and anxiety.
- I have low self-esteem.
- I feel like I don't have much control over my own life.
- I don't feel very optimistic about my future.

If none of these are true for you, you've made a very healthy transition from a bereaved child to adulthood, and the following chapters will show you how you did it. If any, or all, are true for you, don't despair. It's not too late. You see, your parent's death was not an isolated event. It set into motion other changes, other losses, like a row of falling dominoes. It wasn't just the fact of your parent's death that affected you. Three other key variables influenced how you coped, and contributed to who you are today. In the next chapter, we'll take a look at the first of these variables, and you can gauge how much it influenced who you are today.

My Notes

THREE

I Didn't Just Lose My Parent . . .

When my dad died, I didn't just lose him. In some ways, I felt like I lost my mother, too. And there were a lot of other changes. I felt kind of like a pinball shot out of the chute; everywhere I bounced, there was another loss.

—Terrance, thirty-two, reflecting on his father's death when he was eight years old

To understand fully how you were affected by your parent's death, you need to look at what else happened in your life as a result of this loss—what additional changes followed or were set off by your parent's death. How you coped as a child or teen after the death was influenced, not just by the death itself, but also by other changes resulting from this loss. These additional circumstances, like a row of dominoes falling into each other, may have made your healing process even more complicated. And finally, the circumstances surrounding the death and the meaning you made of what happened—what you told yourself about your parent's death—affected you then and continues to influence you now. In this chapter we will look at how other changes, the severity of these additional losses, and the circumstances of the death may have affected your ability to cope.

The Effect of Other Changes

When your parent died, what other changes did you experience?

Here are some of the losses children at The Dougy Center describe encountering after the death of a parent. Check off the changes you experienced following your parent's death:

I Experienced a Lot of Changes in My Daily Routine

Research has indicated that the fewer the changes in daily routine, the better a grieving child or teen will fare. Some of the common changes in daily routine you may have encountered include a shift in your sleeping arrangements, bedtime, mealtimes, or other activities. Some surviving parents allow their child or children to sleep with them following the death of a parent. I'm not suggesting that this is necessarily a negative thing, but it is a change for the child. Often mealtimes are disrupted, and the daily pattern of the family changes dramatically. In addition, activities you may have enjoyed with your deceased parent are no longer available or enjoyable. Fifteen-year-old Shera described how she no longer enjoyed playing softball without her mother to cheer her on. Her seventeen-year-old sister, Cara, however, relished playing basketball and played with a renewed fervor, believing her mother was watching and rooting for her. Either way, the change in previous activities is a frequent reminder of the multiple impacts following the parent's death. What other changes did you experience when your parent died?

In Some Ways I Feel Like I Lost My Surviving Parent Too, At Least for a While, Because He/She Was So Grief-stricken, He/She Couldn't "Be There" for Me

The pain of losing a spouse, coupled with the need to care for children, can be a debilitating combination for many widows or widowers. Some children are almost forced to become a parent to their surviving parent, or to "fill in" as the lost parent. Losing a spouse is emotionally draining, and many parents describe feeling continuously exhausted and distraught in their own grief, with limited emotional reserves left to parent. Others put their own grieving "on hold" as they attempt to meet their children's needs. They may become overprotective, which some children and teens experience as suffocating. Your surviving parent changed as a result of the loss, and many children describe feeling like they'd lost both parents. Are there ways in which you feel like you lost your surviving parent after your parent's death?

You may have lost both parents, either through death or abandonment. You may never have known one of your parents, or the surviving parent may have never been a part of your life. Perhaps you did, literally, parent yourself.

Our Whole Family Changed from How We Related to Each Other Before and After the Death

The loss of one family member leaves a gap resulting in a loss of equilibrium for the entire family, like removing one piece of a mobile unbalances the whole thing. This can change not just daily routines, but the very fabric of how the family members relate to each other. Many children and teens talk about how the family communication patterns changed dramatically, often because they hadn't found a way to talk with each other about how they were coping. Some children and teens "protect" their surviving parent by not mentioning the deceased. And because they are all dealing with unfamiliar emotional territory, in vastly different ways from each other, relationships often became strained. What kinds of changes occurred in your family? If you have siblings, how were those relationships different following your parent's death? How about with your surviving parent?

My Family Fell Apart Completely

Perhaps your family fell apart completely after your parent's death. You may have been raised (or ignored) by relatives or nonrelatives who took you in for unhealthy reasons— for money, because of family pressure, or for live-in help. Your family may have already been dysfunctional or destructive before the death, and things became worse afterwards. You may, literally, have raised yourself.

Did you grow up alone, parent yourself, or find yourself with adults who abused, mistreated, and neglected you?

My Responsibilities in the Family Increased; I Had to Take on More Chores and "Grow Up" Faster

Many bereaved adults talk about how they weren't able to be children after their parent's death, and that the changes required of them, either in responsibilities or in coping with pain at an early age, forced a hypermaturity not experienced by their peers. While this may not necessarily be a bad thing, some adults feel like they sidestepped their childhood. Did you get a chance to be a child? Were you able to enjoy your teen years? Or did you feel like you had been whisked into adulthood before you were ready, or before you should have been expected to be ready?

I Moved into a New Home

Because of financial changes, the need to be closer to other family members, or for other reasons, you may have moved to a different home after your parent's death, perhaps even in another state. This may have made it difficult for you to feel grounded and secure. When a parent dies, it's as if an emotional security rug is pulled out from under you. Piling on other changes, like moving to an entirely new home or environment, may contribute to a sense of helplessness and powerlessness, especially when the circumstances are negative or destructive. Conversely, in rare cases, some children describe moving as a positive change, often because it allowed them to "start over" by being with people who didn't know their history. More frequently, children and teens find that moving following a parent's death is a difficult transition.

I Changed Schools

Whether or not you moved to a new home, you may have changed schools—from elementary school to middle school, or junior high to high school. Like moving to a new home, most children have described the change of school as a difficult transition, with a smaller number describing it as a positive change. It may have been difficult to add yet another challenge to adjust to when you were already faced with so many other changes. Or it may have been a positive change for you, a way to make a fresh start with new friends who didn't treat you differently because you had a parent die. If you changed schools, was this an added difficulty for you?

I Lost Some of My Friends

You may have lost friends because you moved to a new location. Or you may have lost friends because of how they responded to you when your parent died. A lot of adolescents define how friends reacted to their parent's death as a pivotal time in their choice of relationships. "I really got to know who my friends were," says sixteen-year-old Brianna. "It became very clear who cared and who didn't, and I lost some friends when I saw who they really were." The expectations children and teens describe placing on friends varies from person to person—some wanted their friends to treat them exactly as they had prior to the death and not talk about it; others wanted friends to treat them with extra kindness and help them talk and share their grief. What matters in the long run is not some universal standard of how friends *should* react, but whether or not your friends responded in the way *you* wanted that

made the difference. Were your friends there for you? Did you lose friends because of how they responded?

We Didn't Have as Much Money, So Our Lifestyle Changed

Financial pressures following the death of a parent can place a heavy strain on the family. Sometimes a previously non-working parent has to find employment for the first time. A lot of adolescents fear that they will not be able to fulfill their dream of going to college following their parent's death. Financial stresses and the changes resulting from them can result in additional anxiety and uncertainty about the future. Did financial pressures, realities, or fears add to your concerns as a child or teenager following your parent's death?

Someone New Started Baby-sitting or Taking Care of Us

The loss of a parent sometimes means the addition of new people coming into a child's life. Whether it's new baby-sitters or new caregivers, the adjustment of incorporating new people into your family's life is a change not always welcomed by children or teens.

I Had to Fill a New Role in My Family. I Became the Man (or Woman) of the Family

Too often young boys whose father died or young girls whose mother died are unwittingly placed in the role of the deceased. I've heard many boys and teens talk about how they were told directly, sometimes at their father's funeral, "You're the man of the house now. You're going to have to be strong for your mother." Young girls are also instructed, "You're going to have to take care of your dad now that your mother's gone." Sometimes the surviving parent participates in this role change, whether knowingly or unconsciously. Did you become "the man of the house" or "the woman of the house" after your parent's death? If so, you may have consciously or unconsciously been playing out that role throughout your life. Additionally, firstborn children often relate that they felt increasingly responsible for younger siblings, almost in a parental role, following their parent's death. Were you the oldest child when your parent died? Did you fill in as a substitute parent for your younger sibling or siblings? If so, assuming that role has likely had continuing implications in your relationships with them and others.

I Had a Pet Die

Experiencing a pet's death following your parent's death can be a retraumatizing event. Children (and adults as well) often bond with their pets and receive comfort and assurance from them. Pet death is sometimes minimized in importance in our culture. Whether it's the collective effect of another death, a loss of the animal's special bond, or a combination of these factors, losing a pet is often a painful and disturbing experience, especially on the heels of other losses. Did you lose a beloved pet after your parent died?

I Experienced Other Deaths in My Family

It's known as "bereavement overload" when multiple losses make the world feel unsafe and unpredictable. Seventeen-year-old Bryan, whose father and mother died within six months of each other from cancer and a heart attack, respectively, said he felt like everyone around him was going to die. "I felt like anyone I loved or cared about was at risk, and that the world was indifferent, unfriendly, and uncaring." Some children wonder if they're "jinxed" when they experience multiple deaths in their family. Have you carried this concern or fear?

I Had a Friend Die

Another form of bereavement overload can occur when the death of a friend follows the death of a parent. Some young people describe being afraid to love or care about anyone because they fear they will be taken away. A friend's death also highlights your own vulnerability. You may be able to rationalize the death of someone older than you, but when it's someone your own age, a new realization dawns. Did you have a friend or friends die after your parent's death?

My Parent Started Dating

Although some children and adolescents welcome their parent dating or finding a new partner, for many this new development can feel like a betrayal of the deceased parent or a betrayal of the children. This is especially true if they don't like the new person. It may feel like you or your deceased parent is being replaced, or that your parent won't have time for you anymore. Was this part of your experience?

My Parent Remarried

This change can really upset the applecart, especially in blended families. Even if the new stepparent does not bring

NEVER THE SAME

children to the marriage, he or she brings new habits and ideas that must be dealt with. Many children express resentment toward a new "parent" and refuse to accept discipline or "parenting" from them. In some situations, children are happy to have a new mother or father, and embrace them as such, particularly if the deceased parent was abusive or emotionally absent. But the addition of a new family member or members inherently forces a change in roles and atmosphere. If your parent remarried, how did you respond?

My Siblings and I Were Separated from Each Other

In every situation I've encountered where siblings were separated from each other following a parent's death, the change was not experienced by the children as a positive one, even if prior to the death they didn't get along. The loss of their parent may have made them realize how important family is. They've said things like, "We were all we had when our parent died," and "We got closer after the death because we had to depend on each other in ways we didn't have to before." Older siblings may feel responsible for the problems of younger siblings, as if they didn't do enough to ensure they were going to be okay. Younger siblings may feel abandoned or betrayed by older siblings whom they perceive (accurately or not) as not looking out for them. Were you separated from your siblings after your parent's death?

If you checked off a number of these changes, your healing process may have been complicated by the number and severity of these other losses. It's difficult enough to have a parent die; when everything else changes as well, it's hard to get your bearings. Research has indicated that the greater the number of changes that follow a parent's death, the greater impact this has on the healing process.[1] The collective impact of multiple losses can be devastating, especially for children.

Many people don't realize that change, in and of itself, is loss. All changes are losses, even if they provide new opportunities or are experienced as positive changes. Whether we perceive a specific change as a good one, or a bad one, it is still a loss of *something,* even if something better is gained. Death is seldom interpreted as a positive change, even when we may have some sense of relief that the person is out of their suffering. A change like switching jobs may be easier when we choose to switch jobs versus getting fired, but there is still something left behind, trade-offs, and therefore a period of imbalance, instability, and uncertainty. When changes occur that are beyond our control, we experience imbalance and try to "right" ourselves with whatever means we have available. We try to regain our equilibrium and our sense of security. Death is the big im-balancer for children as well as adults. It pulls the rug out from under us, and it takes time and healing to regain our footing. If you experienced a lot of changes following your parent's death, you may fall into one of the two camps I've commonly heard described by adults buffeted by numerous changes after their parent's death when they were children.

One camp, explained by thirty-nine-year-old Rose, is terrified of change: "I felt like nothing was ever stable and never would be, so as an adult I find myself needing con-stancy and reliability from my friends, family, and those around me. I hate change and resist it." At the opposite end of the spectrum is fifty-two-year-old Mark, who be-lieves that "having to constantly readjust to change after my father's death as a child turned out to be a positive for me in that I feel like I can handle anything that comes my way. I kind of thrive on change, actually, and if things are too stable I start to get bored." Either of these polarities can have positive as well as negative consequences, de-pending on how you interpret them. We'll look later at how your response to change may be playing out in your life now, and whether it hinders or helps you.

How the Circumstances of the Death Influence Healing

The circumstances surrounding your parent's death also played a factor in how you coped with this life-changing event. See if any of the following events were part of your experience.

Sudden and Unexpected Death Versus an Anticipated Death

Some studies have indicated that a sudden unexpected death may be experienced as more traumatic for some children because of the unanticipated nature of the loss. "One minute she was here, and the next she was gone," said ten-year-old Bryan, following his mother's death in a car accident. "There was no time to say good-bye, no time for apologies, or anything."

Other studies indicate that some children have a more difficult time following a parent's death from a lengthy illness, especially if the illness resulted in the parent's mental, physical, and emotional deterioration. Because so much of the family's time and energy is dissipated through coping with the increasing decline of the parent, there frequently is not much time or energy left to deal with the children's needs emotionally or physically. And many children report difficulty in watching their parent deteriorate and become someone different from the person they knew. It can be hard to remember the good times, or to remember the parent as a healthy, vibrant person. Some children are excluded from the truth when a parent is terminally ill, and that kind of family secrecy makes them feel unimportant, devalued, and cheated.

The important issue here is not to endlessly debate whether it's worse to have a parent die suddenly or over a period of time, but to recognize that how your parent died impacted you. What was your particular situation, and how did those circumstances affect you then?

Suicide or Homicide

Working since 1986 with children whose parent died by suicide or homicide, I've observed that as a whole they have additional hurdles to confront in their healing process. Both involve law enforcement, carry stigma, and a sense that "if only" something had gone differently, their death may have been prevented.

Suicide

Although it is not uncommon for family members to ask why a family member had to die, this question is usually heightened for those left behind when a suicide occurs.

Often guilt, shame, and anger are intensified as they struggle with wondering if there was something they could have done to prevent the suicide, or whether they contributed in some way to the parent's hopelessness. While interviewing children ages six to sixteen for my doctoral dissertation on the impact of a parent's suicide on children, I asked each one if they thought there was something they could have done to prevent the suicide. Every one had some affirmative answer. "I could have tried harder to make him happy." "I should have bought all the tickets on the plane when he flew to Montana, because I knew he was depressed and it wasn't a good place for him to go." "If I had only asked him to pick me up after school at *this* time, maybe I could have saved him." Additionally, a continuing social stigma toward families of suicide victims contributes to their sense of alienation and isolation. They feel, and often are, judged as bad families, crazy families, or sick families. I think it's a defense mechanism people use to protect themselves from the thought that a suicide could happen in their family, but our society in general does not provide much support or consolation to children and adults bereaved by suicide. If your parent died by suicide, have you felt shame or embarrassment about this?

Often children or teens wonder if they are "fated" to die by suicide; if it is in their genes. There *is* some support for a higher frequency of suicides in those whose parent suicided, that it "runs in the family." You may have a higher susceptibility for suicide if your parent suicided, for two reasons. First, your parent set an example that suicide was a way out of pain. Second, there is much medical evidence for chemical contributors to suicide, that is, in layperson's terms, a person's brain is not functioning properly. Yet our society casts judgment on those whose brains—a human organ—are not working correctly in ways it does not judge those whose other organ failures—kidneys, lungs, heart—result in their death, even when their own behaviors, like alcohol abuse and smoking, contribute to their death. Chemical imbalances, like alcoholism, are in part genetic. Therefore, in that sense, susceptibility for suicide may be higher in children who've had a parent suicide just like some children are more at risk for heart disease, breast cancer, or diabetes because of their parent's histories. This, however, does not mean one is "fated" to suicide, or that it is inevitable.

Edwin Shneidman, a prominent suicidologist who studied the subject for over forty-five years, writes compellingly in *The Suicidal Mind*[2] and *Suicide as Psychache*,[3] that ultimately a suicide occurs when three factors collide: The first is when a person reaches the limit of their threshold for psychological pain, resulting in their inability to envision any escape from pain other than death. The second is when they have ready access to instruments of suicide—guns, knives, pills. And the third is what he calls "perturbation," an agitated state when they perceive that their discomfort and anxiety is intolerable. If all three conditions coincide, a suicide attempt is inevitable—not necessarily unpreventable, but inevitable. To reduce the threat, at least one of the three conditions has to be reduced. That is, their psychological pain level must be reduced, or their access to tools of self-destruction must be stopped, or their level of anxiety must be lessened.

You may notice that I have not used the common terminology "committed suicide." It's because I believe this phrase incorrectly and unfairly accuses the suicide victim of an act over which they had no control. (If they had control, they would not have suicided. If they had in other words, been in their right mind, they would not have taken their life.) The topic of "rational suicide" or physician-assisted suicide/Death with Dignity, as in the case of debilitating terminal illness, is a whole other topic of its own and outside the scope of these comments. The word "commit" is frequently paired with negatively judged acts: commit adultery, commit murder, commit a crime, commit a felony. I strongly believe that because the suicidal person's mind is not working properly, there is a moment where suicide is no longer a choice—when all three contributing factors collide at a heightened level. If at that moment the person has access to the means to die, the suicide will happen. If at that moment the person is prevented from suiciding because he or she does not have the means, the suicide can be prevented. People refer to suicide as an "easy way out," but if you think about it, would it be easy for someone who is thinking clearly to slit their wrist, jump off of a bridge, or pull the trigger of a gun?

If your parent died by suicide, you may have struggled with suicidal thoughts yourself. This is not unusual. But know that if such feelings overwhelm you, you can and should ask for help. You may be susceptible to depression or feelings of wanting to die through a chemical imbalance, but you are not fated to die in this way just because your parent did. Even if you have not had suicidal thoughts, the social stigma of a parent's suicide probably has added to your difficulty in healing from this loss and its impact on your life.

Homicide

Similar to the loss of a parent by suicide, a death by homicide is often stigmatized by our society. I believe there is a human tendency to protect ourselves from the possibility that bad things can happen to us, and often people assume that murders happen to "bad people who are doing bad things in bad places." In addition to the general stigma, there are many other complications when someone dies by homicide, including from a drunk driving crash. (Notice I do not say drunk driving "accident." I support the stand of MADD, Mothers Against Drunk Driving, who assert that driving drunk is not an accident, but rather a choice.

If your parent was killed DWI, driving while intoxicated, you may have a double load of stigma to deal with, especially if anyone else died in the crash.) Homicide deaths are preventable, and therefore guilt and "if onlys" frequently haunt those left behind.

The media and the legal system do not always provide truth or justice in the minds of the survivors. And ultimately, true justice is impossible because no matter what the verdict, the deceased's life cannot be restored. If your parent was murdered, you had many additional stresses to deal with, including a prolonged period of uncertainty and lack of closure as the legal system involvement dragged on. If the perpetrator was not found, you have a continued lack of resolution to that aspect of the crime. Even if the perpetrator died or was sentenced to prison, most child survivors of a parent's homicide continue to believe the person will someday get out and get them, or fear that someone else will kill them.

Understandably, feelings of anger and desire for revenge often are experienced by the survivors of a homicide. When those feelings cannot be channeled constructively or transformed into positive action, they can be consuming and damaging.

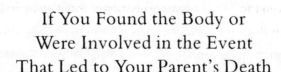

If You Found the Body or
Were Involved in the Event
That Led to Your Parent's Death

Sixteen-year-old Jennifer returned home from school to find her mother dead of a self-inflicted gunshot wound. Jason, ten, discovered his father's body in his bed one morning, the victim of a heart attack. These images may be difficult to get out of your mind and can significantly interfere with your ability to heal. In extreme cases, Post-traumatic Stress Disorder (PTSD) may result in experiencing flashbacks, and other serious difficulties.

Similarly, if you were involved in the circumstances that resulted in your parent's death, you may have additional hurdles on your path toward healing. Seventeen-year-old Iko was twelve when she and her mother were buried under a beam in their home's collapse in the Kobe, Japan, earthquake in January 1996. For six hours, trapped and unable to move, she heard her mother's moans and cries for help before they were rescued. Her mother died en route to the hospital. Not only did Iko have her own serious physical injuries to deal with, she was unable to rid her memory of her mother's cries and her own helplessness in preventing her mother's death. Suffering panic attacks and anxiety, Iko was severely retriggered when terrorist-controlled planes crashed into the World Trade Center Buildings on September 11,

2001, even though she was thousands of miles away in Japan. These kinds of retriggering events, though not uncommon, may require professional help to work through. There is a difference between negative triggering events or flashbacks, and memory recalls, or what psychologist Alan Wolfelt calls "memory embraces." Remembering or reliving scenes is common following a death; if these scenes are consistently troubling or interfere with living, a competent therapist may help.

Your Relationship to the Deceased

Another factor that influenced how you coped with your parent's death is the relationship you had with your parent prior to the death. For those who had conflicted relationships or unresolved business, the complications in healing are increased. Seventeen-year-old Danielle's father was emotionally and sexually abusive. Several months after he was convicted of the abuse, he died. In her mind, her father's abuse resulted in his death. However, she had conflicting feelings about her role in his death. At times she expressed that if she hadn't told on him, he might still be alive, so she felt guilt and self-blame. Other times she was glad he was gone because she was no longer being abused. When she felt glad he was gone, she then felt guilty because she'd been told "it isn't good to think badly of someone who's dead." That cycle of conflicting feelings kept her stuck in ways of thinking and feeling that were destructive.

Other children describe a last encounter with the parent prior to the death that fills them with regret. Ten-year-old Joseph had an argument with his father the night before he died, and he was consumed by feelings of regret about not being able to apologize. He, too, experienced guilt, and made a connection between the fight and his father's death, even though there was no logical connection between the two events. If your parents were divorced, separated, or unhappy together, you may have felt (as many children do) that you somehow contributed to their unhappiness. If your last encounter with your parent was negative, or you had unresolved concerns when they died, your healing was probably more complicated after their death.

As you reflect on the additional losses and circumstances of your parent's death as discussed in this chapter, remember that losing your parent was a life-altering event in and of itself. The additional changes it set into motion changed the course of your life. The number of changes, severity of other losses, and specific circumstances of the death added additional layers to the already difficult challenge of coping and healing. Next, we will look at the second of the three variables affecting how you coped: the influence, positive and negative, of those around you, how they handled your parent's death, and how this influenced you as a child.

My Notes

My Notes

How Others Influenced
Your Grieving

The second major influence on how you coped as a child following your parent's death, as well as how you now cope as an adult, was drilled home to me yesterday as I responded to media requests following a tragic event in the city where I live. The estranged husband of a twenty-three-year-old woman entered her apartment and shot her in the head in front of their two daughters, three and five. When the police broke in shortly thereafter, he turned the gun on himself. Two little girls are now left without a mother or father, and with the memory of those violent acts. Reporters' questions flowed with three common concerns: Are these girls too young to remember this event? If not, what will they remember? And what are the odds for them to have healthy lives given this major trauma?

In chapter 5, we will look in more detail at their first questions—how the age of a child and the corresponding developmental tasks and abilities influences their understanding, memory, and ability to cope. But the short answer to the question of whether young children remember traumatic events is yes. Just because they can't verbalize thoughts or feelings at the time doesn't mean they aren't absorbing impressions. What they remember, how they reconstruct it through the lens of time and memory, and how they are able (or unable) to verbalize this reconstruction depends on numerous factors.

In the previous chapter we looked at the influence of other changes, the severity of additional losses, and how the circumstances of the death may have impacted you. Now, we'll explore a second major influence: how those around you handled your parent's death, and how their responses have affected you, for better and for worse. The answers to the reporters' second and third questions about these two little girls—What will they remember? and What are the odds for them to have healthy lives?—will be shaped in large part by what those around them do and fail to do. The same was true for you. You've probably heard the saying that it takes a village to raise a child. A village can also ruin a child!

It's important before exploring this topic more fully to

understand that none of these factors *determines* outcome. I'm not suggesting that how you are in your adult life is set in concrete because of what happened to you or how others responded. Rather, you have been *shaped and influenced* by these events, by how others responded, by how you were treated, and by the sense you made of it then and now. You didn't have a choice about losing your mother or father. You didn't have much say in how others responded to you. You had limited though developing ability to cope as a child and teen. And as an adult, you have complete choice now about how you want to feel, think, and act. It may not seem like it at times, but the stories you tell yourself, and the meaning you make of them, in large part do determine your outcome. So hang on, and let's look at how others influenced your grieving. If you can recognize these influences and understand how they helped set you on a course, you can decide, even now, how you choose to let them affect the quality of your life.

The Influence of Your Family and Surviving Parent

As may be expected, for the majority of children and teens, the most influential person in your life following your parent's death was your surviving parent. There's an exception to this, of course, if both of your parents died, or if the nondeceased parent was not a part of your life. If your parent died and you didn't know your other parent, or you had a succession of parent figures through foster care or moving from relative to relative, these additional losses, as discussed previously, complicated your healing process. Perhaps a "parent figure" or "parent figures" stood in for that role. They may have been positive or destructive forces in your life. Whether your parent or parent figure(s) was healthy or unhealthy, you were strongly influenced by them.

Before we look more closely at how your surviving parent influenced you, let's take a glance at your family back then as a system. Prior to your parent's death, your family, like all families, had a structure, rules (verbalized or not verbalized), traditions, and ways of doing things, a pecking order, and other characteristics unique to your particular unit. It may have been a generally healthy family, or it may have been a generally unhealthy family. Unhealthy families don't tend to become healthier following a traumatic event, and although it's not impossible, it's rare. Healthy families have a better chance of remaining healthy following a trauma, but these events put a tremendous strain on even the best of systems. When your parent died, or even before the death, if he or she suffered an injury or disease, your family experienced a major jolt to its system.

Think of the members of your family as a hanging mobile. Each person played a role that kept the mobile balanced. This doesn't necessarily mean the family was balanced in a healthy way, but there was an agreement, spoken or not, about roles, responsibilities, and the respective weight each person carried. Many events can occur to set the mobile off balance. How the family restores that equilibrium following stressful events will color how each person in the family develops. When your parent died, the family mobile lost one of its key players, and the entire mobile was thrown off balance. How did your family recreate that mobile, that family structure, without your parent? Was it in a way that fostered health, or in a way that contributed to alienation? Did your family mobile rebalance, or were some or all of the players cut out completely?

TALK ABOUT DADDY

One of the pioneers in family systems therapy, Virginia Satir, found that healthy families had four characteristics: high self-worth; direct, clear, specific, and honest communication; flexible, appropriate rules; and an open and hopeful attitude toward society.[1] Troubled families exhibited the opposite traits: low self-worth; indirect, vague, and dishonest communication; rigid, nonnegotiable rules; and a blaming, fearful attitude toward society.

No

If your family was troubled prior to the death, chances are that it didn't get much healthier after the death. It may have completely fallen apart. If your family was healthy prior to the death, it still faced major challenges in these four areas among others. Individual self-worth and the collective self-worth of a family may be shaken in the face of catastrophe. Communication following a death frequently leans toward indirectness, vagueness, and dishonesty as even the best intentioned parent struggles with what to share and what not to share with the children. Because the death has literally resulted in a new family, a new mobile, by definition the rules have to change. And depending on the circumstances of the death and the response of extended family, friends, and the community, one's attitude toward others is usually challenged. Even the most open and hopeful families can be strained as well-meaning but uninformed (or sometimes ill-meaning well-informed or uninformed) people struggle to respond.

It's a given that the stress on your family increased following your parent's death. Even in situations where the death afforded the family some relief, there was stress simply due to change. Your surviving parent may have been divorced from your other parent. Your family may have been chaotic coping with a parent dying from a lengthy and prolonged illness. Your parent may have been abusive, addicted, emotionally distant, with their death actually resulting in some sense of relief. But in any case, your family experienced increased stress following your parent's death. In the Harvard Child Bereavement Study, comparing parentally bereaved children between six and seventeen to children who did not experience a parent's death, one of the areas explored by J. William Worden and Phyllis Rolfe Silverman was the stressors more commonly found in families where a parent had died.[2] There were seven. Parentally bereaved children experienced more conflict among themselves. There were more family members with emotional problems, and the abuse of alcohol and other drugs was more prevalent. They reported increased arguments between parents and children, and more unsolved problems than nonbereaved families. Not surprisingly, a source of conflict was chores that did not get done. There was also an increase in conflict with in-laws and other relatives. Obviously these stressors place even more tension on an already fragile system.

Your Surviving Parent's Reaction

Given the change in the family dynamics following your parent's death, it probably comes as no great surprise to you that your surviving parent's reaction was one of the most influential forces on you as a child or teen. In the Harvard Child Bereavement Study, the emotional well-being of the widowed parent clearly affected how the children were doing. Surviving parents who reported greater depression, financial difficulties, less effective coping, lack of support, and inability to share their feelings satisfactorily had children who were more depressed, anxious, withdrawn, with more health problems and greater emotional and behavioral difficulties. If you didn't have a surviving parent, your challenges were also complicated, whether you grew up with loving, supportive, and healthy parent substitutes, or unhealthy ones, deeply influenced you.

A large part of healthy parenting is nurturing, promoting, and sustaining children's healthy growth and development. In a very broad categorization, I've seen surviving parents tend toward one of three parenting styles following a death: Overnurturing, undernurturing, and appropriate nurturing. Of course no parent is the perfect parent, displaying appropriate nurturing every minute of the day in every circumstance. But because of the added pressures and anxiety following a death, some parents may fall into one of the extremes more frequently than they had previous to the death. Or their parenting style prior to the death may have tended toward under- or overnurturing, in which case it most likely steered even further in that direction.

Overnurturing is an understandable reaction to the loss of someone close to you. When someone we know dies, we have an increased and heightened understanding of the fragility and brevity of life. When you realize that someone can be taken from you in an instant, most of us respond by pulling those we love closer to us. That natural response may become unhealthy if a parent smothers a child or teen, places new and overly restrictive requirements or rules on them, or unconsciously spoils the child in an effort to "make up" for the loss he or she has suffered. Overnurtured children, whom Jungian analyst James Hollis defines as "overwhelmed," have difficulties with boundaries, tend to be defensive and passive, and are codependent.[3]

Undernurturing results in another set of problems for children. Parents who were already distant, or who become emotionally and/or physically distant may be incapacitated by their own depression or grief and unable to adequately promote and sustain their child's healthy development. Sometimes this is a temporary situation as the acute shock and numbness of a death may paralyze the surviving parent. Other times, it's a continuation of the predeath parenting style. Sometimes the bereaved spouse unconsciously places a child in the role of the deceased. Undernurtured bereaved children tend to engage in dependent patterns and relationships in what Hollis calls "an addictive search for a more positive Other."[4] They may also appear incapable of sustaining intimacy in relationships for fear of abandonment. You may have been undernurtured by your surviving parent. If you had no surviving parent, you may have been undernurtured by the parent figure or figures in your life.

So what does appropriate nurturing of a grieving child or teen look like? What do grieving children need from their surviving parent and others in order to grow and develop in healthy ways? First, they need the same things all children need. Additionally, they need these qualities and actions applied to them as grieving children. As you read the following list, think about which of these you received support around and which you didn't.

Ten Needs of Grieving Children

1. Good Modeling

Grieving children and teens need examples of positive coping behavior from their surviving parent, as well as from the other adults around them. They are taking their cues from the environment, carefully watching and either imitating or rejecting what they see in the actions of others. Parents at The Dougy Center question frequently how to find a balance between what they feel and what they should show their children. The stoic, bottled-up parent shows children that they should be strong at all costs, keep their feelings inside, and move on. The incapacitated parent who cannot get out of bed and who forces their children into parenting them places an unrealistic and difficult burden on children unprepared for this responsibility. The parent who cries only behind a closed bedroom door, emerging with reddened eyes pretending all is well, implies that crying and sadness cannot be shared. Parents who have adult support systems and who can share their feelings without placing their children in a position of needing to take care of them, exemplify that it's okay to feel, to express feelings, and to ask for help.

Of course, your parent wasn't the only adult whose response you were watching as you explored how to respond to your parent's death. Teachers, school counselors, coaches, clergy, youth workers, aunts, uncles, other relatives, friends' parents, all played a role in shaping how you processed, or failed to process, this pivotal event in your life. Most kids at The Dougy Center have multiple stories about adults who helped them and those who hindered them in the days, weeks, and months after the death.

Thirty years after his father's death, forty-year-old Deighton shared an experience that was engraved in his memory. "My father died on my brother's ninth birthday. I was ten. I still remember people saying all kinds of things, and even then I was wishing they'd just keep their mouths shut. One woman said to me, 'Wasn't it wonderful your father was born into heaven on your brother's birthday?' I just wanted to slug her!"

What adults were there for you when your parent died? If you were of school age, how did your teacher or teachers handle your return to the classroom? If you were part of a religious community, did that community support or abandon you? Was there anyone, any adult, who you can point to who modeled helpful and positive responses following your parent's death? If so, you're fortunate. If not, you may be living out the poor modeling you witnessed many years ago.

2. Honest, Clear Information

It seems so logical that parents and adults should be honest with children, and yet, when it comes to talking about death, there's often a genuine hesitancy to do so. I've come to believe there are four main reasons why adults lie or withhold information from children following a death. All are well-intentioned efforts to do the right thing; all are ultimately unproductive for children. One reason is that their own fear, grief, disbelief, and other thoughts and feelings interfere. If I, as a parent, can't understand why my husband died in a car wreck, by suicide, or was stricken with cancer, how can I possibly explain it to my children? Even though death is the universal experience—100 percent of us will die—we generally believe it's best when someone has lived a full life into their eighties or nineties and drifts off painlessly in their sleep. When children are "robbed" of a parent in the prime of life, it feels unfair, unnatural, and we are unprepared for it. It challenges our beliefs, blindsides our faith, and crumbles our dreams.

A second reason is that as adults we naturally want to protect children from pain. A couple of weeks after the September 11 terrorist attacks in 2001, I was meeting with groups of parents who worked for a company displaced in the wake of the World Trade Center's collapse. A father shared with me that his nine-year-old daughter, since September 12, had been throwing up and not wanting to go

Example of how smart children are

to sleep, but that he couldn't really associate it with the events of the eleventh because she didn't know about what had happened. He "assumed" she didn't know because they didn't have a television. This was a bright, educated man. I asked if his daughter had been to school since the eleventh and he said yes. When I said, "They're talking about it in school," he replied quietly, "I was hoping they weren't." Imagine the fear and confusion this little girl must have been experiencing with the world outside her home reeling from this huge event, while the conspiracy of silence at home pretended it had not happened. This father's own fear and desire to protect his daughter actually contributed to more pain and confusion for her.

A third reason is that adults often don't know how to talk about death, and especially to children. At The Dougy Center we receive many calls from parents and other adults wanting assistance in knowing how to explain a death to a child. Generally, I ask the person to tell me what happened. When they finish, I usually say "That's what you need to tell your children." Unless the language is too complex for the age of the child, what they tell me is the same thing they can tell their child.

A fourth reason is more subtle, but common. It is very difficult to see someone in pain and not be able to relieve them of that pain. The truth is painful, and we want to spare them, and ourselves, that kind of pain. I've never yet met anyone who was excited and eager to tell a child his father was found dead. At the same time, I have yet to hear a child or teen say they were glad they were lied to about the circumstances of a death.

If you were lied to, or information was withheld from you after your parent's death, you may be carrying some anger and resentment about that. You may have information you still wonder about, and still don't know. It's not too late to find out. And in most cases, adults who lied to you or withheld the truth probably did so because they didn't know any better at the time.

3. To Be Understood

One interesting aspect that the Harvard Child Bereavement Study looked at was how accurately the parent perceived how the child was doing. In situations where the child's perception and the parent's perception were in synch, the child felt more understood and validated, even if both saw the child as having difficulties. If the parent's perception and the child's perception were at odds, the child tended to have more anxiety and other problems.

In my experience with families at The Dougy Center, it's not at all unusual for the children and their parents to misperceive each other. This may happen when parents don't tell the children the truth, and the children either intuit that they're being lied to or know the truth from others. A telling example is nine-year-old Samuel, whose father suicided in his car by inhaling the exhaust fumes. In a well-intentioned attempt to protect Samuel from this harsh reality, his mother told him his father had died in a car accident. Samuel knew from other children, as well as from overheard conversations among adults, that his father had killed himself. In one of his groups, he shared with the other children that his father had died by suicide, but asked them not to tell his mother. "She thinks he was in a car accident," he explained to them.

Often parents cannot accurately assess how their children are doing because they are understandably absorbed in their own grief and doing all they can just to get up each morning. It's also common that the family members "protect" each other by not bringing up difficult thoughts or feelings, sometimes because they simply don't know how, or when they do, a parent withdraws, cries, or reacts in a way the child finds uncomfortable.

When your parent died, did you feel that your surviving parent understood how you were doing? If so, you had a little added boost over those children who did not feel understood by their surviving parent. In the Harvard study, parents who reported greater depression, and who had experienced the sudden, unexpected death of their spouse, tended to be less accurate in perceiving how their children were faring. Some of the consequences of feeling understood by the surviving parent among the population studied were less anxiety and greater trust in one's own feelings, resulting in a stronger sense of internal control. If you have the sense that your parent did not understand you, you may have carried more anxiety, less trust in your own feelings, and a greater sense that events happen to you rather than you having control over them.

4. Inclusion

When your parent died, were you included in discussions and decisions around a memorial service, funeral, or burial arrangements? The funeral industry has come a long way in advising and equipping parents to include their children and offer them choices as to how they'd like to participate. But this is a relatively young concept, and many children and teens are kept completely in the dark in the days following their parent's death. A lot of discussions in our adolescent groups at The Dougy Center revolve around their frustration and anger at being excluded from decisions and discussions. It feels devaluing, they say, like we didn't matter enough to have a say. Among the common questions we receive from callers to our "Information and Referral Phone Line" at the center are those revolving around children's involvement in funerals. Should children attend or not? Should they see "the body"? In every case, the advice we give is to allow the child or teen informed choice. If they have accurate, clear information, and are permitted to make their own choice, they fare better than those children or teens who are forced into decisions over which they have no say or control. We should not assume we know what is best for a child, or how he or she is processing the death. The following example illustrates good handling of this issue and the power of choice:

A woman's ex-husband and their two young sons were killed in a car accident, leaving one surviving child, seven-year-old Shanna. Shanna wanted to see her brothers and father before they were cremated, and her mother agonized over what to do, enlisting the advice of friends and professionals. The recommendations were about 60/40, with most people suggesting the lingering memory of them in caskets would not be a good thing for Shanna. Everyone had an opinion. Her mother received the wise advice to talk to Shanna about it. To explain her concerns and fear that Shanna might have a bad memory after seeing them, rather than remembering them alive, laughing and playing. She also gave Shanna information about how they would look different from how she knew them alive, and in what ways, what the setting of the funeral home would be, and that she could change her mind at any time about whatever decision she made. Shanna took in all the information and said she definitely wanted to see them. She explained that "if I died, and they didn't come to see me and say good-bye, I would be so mad!" She did see them, was proud of her decision, and speaks of it today, several years later, as one of the best memories she has. Her mother had the wisdom to provide her with the information, express her own concerns, and allow her to choose.

When your parent died, were you invited to be involved in any of the following decisions or discussions?

- Whether to cremate or bury.
- What casket to select.
- What your deceased parent would wear.
- Placing something in the casket.
- What kind of service to hold, if any.
- Whether or not to attend a service.
- Participating in a service.

If you had choice in these matters, and your choices were respected, your experience was fortunate, and unfortunately, somewhat rare.

5. A Sense of Control

As adults, when a death occurs, we are swept into an unfamiliar world with new language and unclear rules. For children and teens, that world holds even more uncertainty and unknowns. Additionally, we all feel a kind of helplessness in the face of death. There was nothing we could do to prevent it, and we recognize our powerlessness. This helplessness and powerlessness in children can translate later into an overwhelming sense that one does not have control over one's own existence. While we generally don't have a say and control over the circumstances of our death (except in the case of suicide), as well as in many aspects of our lives, we still do have choice about how we will respond to what happens to us and in us. As we saw in chapter 2, parentally bereaved children tend to have a higher external locus of control, which can play itself out in adulthood as a victim stance, in searching for the "perfect other" who will make our life complete, and other nonproductive behaviors. One of the best pieces of advice I can give to those parenting a grieving child or teen is to find and permit opportunities for them to regain that lost sense of control. Unfortunately, in an effort to regain control, parents often swing to one of two extremes—tightening the reins on their children out of fear or allowing full rein as a way of "compensating" for their loss.

When your parent died, did you feel like your life was out of control? What did your surviving parent do to help you regain a sense of control and stability? What did you do to try to regain your equilibrium? If you can't answer these questions, you may still be operating in life from a place of external control, being controlled not from within, but by those around you. We'll look at this in more detail later, as well as what you can do about it now.

6. *Consistency*

So many things change after a parent's death, especially if the deceased parent was living with you at the time of his or her death. If your parents were divorced and you did not live with the parent who died, your day-to-day changes may have been fewer than they'd been if you lived together. Either way, your world was rocked and changed, and one of the ways that could help you restore balance was for your surviving parent to stay consistent and minimize other changes in your life to the best of his or her ability. As previously discussed, many widowed parents who are raising their children alone for the first time become lax or overrestrictive in applying rules and discipline. The Harvard Child Bereavement Study, among others, found that bereaved children and adolescents whose surviving parent did not provide consistency in discipline were more aggressive, had less impulse control, and exhibited more behavioral problems.

Did your parent's parenting style, particularly in the boundaries and rules set for you, change following your parent's death? If they were stricter, or more lax, you may have chafed under the imposed change. If you were raised by someone other than a parent, how did their child-rearing styles affect you?

7. A Sense of Security and Safety

Death by definition shakes one's sense of safety and security, especially if the death was violent or seen as preventable. One of the first things young children wonder about after a parent's death is *What will happen to me?* Frequently young children, as well as older ones, regress in their behaviors. Toddlers who were potty trained wet the bed and demand bottles. Not uncommonly, children become clingy, afraid for the safety of their remaining parent, and aware in a new way not only that everyone will die, but that it can happen at any time.

If your parent died violently, you probably, like the kids in The Dougy Center's "Healing from a Murder" groups, had fears and concerns for your own safety, even if the perpetrator was caught and behind bars. You may have generalized that fear to a strong sense of feeling unsafe in the world, even later as an adult.

If your parent suicided, you may wonder, as many of those in The Dougy Center's "Healing from a Suicide" groups do, whether you also are "fated" to die by suicide, whether it is in your genes. You may have struggled over the years with depression or a generalized sense of meaninglessness. You may have felt (and probably were) ostracized and judged by those around you for having a parent die by suicide.

If your parent died from a disease or illness, you may have had fears (and still have fear) that you would also get the disease or not live past the age of your parent's death.

None of these fears are uncommon among children and adolescents. Nor are they uncommon among adults who had a parent die when they were children. There may be ways in which you have carried insecurity and fear, unknowingly, into your adult years. There may be ways in which this fear is preventing you from having the full and rich life you could have, even now. Many of your fears may have a legitimate basis. You may in fact have susceptibility to the disease that took your parent's life. If you were mistreated or abused in your living situation following your parent's death, your fear, insecurity, and anxiety may be well-founded. However, you do not have to remain a victim of those who mistreated you. You don't have to live out of fear and protection.

8. Permission to Express (or Not)

One of the comments children and teens commonly make about why they like attending The Dougy Center is that they have a safe place to express, or not express, their thoughts and feelings. As we'll see in a later chapter when we explore the role of expression in healing and the misconceptions about correct ways to grieve, there is no one right way for expressions of grief to emerge. Prior to your parent's death, you may have been quiet and not particularly verbal, and you may have remained so. You may have been outgoing and gregarious and continued to be so. Or you may have changed how you expressed yourself after this loss. Either way, what you needed at that time was permission to express, as well as to take a break from expressing, how you felt. Children who feel pressured to talk, or cry, or show emotion will likely withdraw even further. That's why one of very few rules, all geared to safety, at The Dougy Center is the "I pass" rule. It means that no one is ever forced to talk, forced to share, or made to participate in any activity they don't want to. In that process, choice and control are strengthened, the individual needs of children and teens are respected, and each person's process is valued.

Not all children cry; not all children verbalize. Some children barely show any outside effect as a result of their parent's death. That may mean they're coping with it privately in ways that are working just fine for them, or it may mean they don't feel safe, or don't know how, to share with others. Either way, forcing will be ineffectual.

Think back to the time after your parent's death. Did you have permission from those around you to do what you needed to do, to express how you felt as you needed? Or were you surrounded by adults who told you to "get over it," "put it behind you," or "move on"? Did you have the freedom to talk or not talk? If you had choices, and made choices you felt good about, you are fortunate. Every day we hear many stories at The Dougy Center about how alone children felt after their parent's death, and how they felt either forced or not encouraged to express themselves.

9. *Avenues to Express*

Perhaps you had permission to express yourself, or at least didn't feel that you were being discouraged to do so, but you really didn't know how. Welcome to the club! Mainstream American society does a very poor job, I believe, in encouraging or accepting ritual and expressions for grieving beyond the funeral or memorial service. Working adults get three days of funeral leave and return to work where coworkers frequently ignore them out of fear of saying the wrong thing. Children return to school and the routines of life without constructive ways to express their feelings of anger, fear, rage, relief, guilt, and anxiety, among others.

Thinking back, do you remember what you did to express how you felt in the weeks and months after your parent's death? Was there someone you could talk to? Did you express yourself through art, play, sports? At The Dougy Center, we provide a variety of opportunities for children and teens to express themselves if they choose to, ranging from mask making, painting, chalk, clay work, physical (and cerebral) games, to our "Volcano Room," a padded safe room where they can hit a punching bag, tumble, throw pillows and stuffed animals, and get out the energy they're so frequently being told by adults to keep inside. A lot of the kids at the center, we're told, have behavioral problems, sometimes referred to as "acting out." Often, their "behavioral problems" are really adults' "perception problems" and their "acting out" is a young person's way of saying, "Look at me; I need help!" Too often, instead of attending to their needs, children are ostracized by adults and other kids, which only perpetuates the cycle.

All kids "act out" what's inside of them. Adults do, too, if you really think about it. We're all acting out what is inside of us, the accumulated hurts and pains, the successes, fears, and hopes. It's part of being human. As James Hollis states in a simple yet true reductionism, "All behavior is anxiety management." We're all "acting out" all the time in ways that will relieve our anxiety and keep us safe. Children do so out of a sense of necessity because the world is so much bigger than them, and they have so little say in it. As we age, we find ways to cope, but that scared child is still inside all of us. Have you found ways to express yourself, or are you still carrying your fears and concerns bottled up inside? If they're still in there, unexpressed, they'll wait. But they will not remain silent forever.

10. *Memorialization, Connection, and Meaning Making*

This may be the least understood need of the griever—the need to stay connected in some way to the deceased and to make sense of or meaning around what happened, why your parent had to die. In a culture that tells us to "move on" after a death, there is little recognition of or appreciation for the need to continue a relationship with the deceased. When your father or mother died, even if your parent remarried, the deceased parent was the only biological father or mother you would ever have. Unless you were one of those kids who was happy and relieved when your parent died, usually as a result of abuse or neglect, you may not have felt a need to stay connected. But you still had the need to make meaning of what happened. But for most children and adolescents, there is a strong desire not to forget and to "stay in touch with" the deceased parent. Because it's not particularly encouraged by our society, these methods often remain private, though they're shared frequently with their peers in support groups at places like The Dougy Center.

Memorialization may be as "simple" as finding ways to mark anniversaries, birthdays, Father's Day or Mother's Day, and the anniversary of your parent's death. It may mean visiting a special place or a grave site. It may include talking to photos, writing letters to your deceased parent, visiting him or her in dreams, or having a real sense that they are watching you, rooting for you. You may have been encouraged, or discouraged, as a child or teen, to find ways of staying connected with your deceased parent. You may have thought such experiences were strange, or "crazy," but they're actually very common. In what ways, after your parent's death, did you memorialize or stay connected to your deceased parent? In what ways, if any, do you do so now?

In addition to memorialization and connection with the deceased is the importance of finding meaning in their death. What sense did you make of your parent's death at the time? Did you believe you were robbed, that life was random and unfair? Did you make some kind of spiritual sense out of the loss? Did you question why and why you? Did it challenge your core beliefs or force you to develop some?

Here's what one man told me, reflecting back on his father's death when he was ten. "My understanding of God changed fundamentally after my father died. I grew up believing God had a plan, that he made everything happen. If you had a car accident, dropped the groceries, it was all part of God's plan. When my father died I couldn't make any sense of why. He died for no reason; it couldn't fit into a plan. I developed a clear understanding that God didn't necessarily have a plan. If he was there at all, he was just watching. I wasn't mad at him; I was more resigned, like, oh, I get it now, I was mistaken. There's no plan. . . ."

On the opposite side of the fence, fifty-three-year-old Damen shared with me that after his father's death when he was thirteen "I struggled for a while with how God could let this happen, and why my dad was taken from me. The whole 'why me' thing. Over time and a lot of soul-searching and study, I decided that I was not immune to pain or hurt, and that I could look at it like God had a special plan for me, that I could be stronger as a result of this setback. I've missed having a dad the whole rest of my life, but I think I've been more sensitive and caring as a result, and I believe that someday I'll see my dad again. I grew up faster than other kids I knew, but I have been successful and somewhat driven, and I attribute a lot of that to not having a father, having to get out there on my own."

What meaning, if any, do you make of your parent's death now? Later, we'll explore how your response to this question influences you in ways you may not be aware of.

Before we close this chapter and look at how your age and developmental abilities at the time of your parent's death influenced you, let's take a brief look at the influence of some other pivotal people in your life. We've discussed how your surviving parent's response influenced you, and the needs you had from him or her and other adults in your world. There's also the influence of your siblings, if you had any, as well as extended family.

The Influence of Siblings and Extended Family

If you were an only child when your parent died, you obviously didn't have the influence of siblings to cope with. But you have some issues that those with siblings didn't. Perhaps wishing your parent had lived so that you could have a brother or sister. Perhaps resenting (or reveling in) so much focus on you as the only child of the deceased.

If you had siblings, you may have banded together and assumed protective roles toward each other. More commonly, I see siblings polarize and become more distant as they struggle to deal with their own grief, and perhaps their individual beliefs and assumptions about how their siblings are doing or "should" respond. Often these behaviors are carried into adult relationships with siblings. All children in families assume roles. When a parent dies, those roles may be redefined, as in the case of the oldest serving as a substitute parent, or the only boy assuming a "father" role, or the only girl assuming a "mother" role. How did you and your siblings relate to each other after your parent's death? Were you helpful, harmful, or benign? And how has that carried over to your relationships as adults? Were you separated from your siblings? Do you need to find them, or reach out to attempt renewed relationships?

Extended family can also be a source of support or a source of difficulty. If your grandparents, the parents of your deceased parent, were involved in your life at the time, their support or withdrawal may have helped or hurt you. Was there a special aunt or uncle who reached out to you, who substituted as a role model for your mother or father? Who was there, and who failed to be there, who taught you something about family and influenced you?

Were there other significant adults in your life at the time of your parent's death? They may have been significant because they helped you or because they failed to help you. Do you remember specific adults who were "there for you" outside of your family? If you do, you discovered one of the key sources of resilience in children. We'll take a closer look at how you coped and survived in chapter 6, but for now, see if you can name any adults you remember being supportive to you after your parent died. If there were no adults who helped or supported you, note that. If you were your own and only support system, you have truly bucked the odds.

The Influence of Friends

Finally, if you were of school age when your parent died, what was it like going back, and how were you treated by your friends? Here's how some of the kids at The Dougy Center responded to this question:

"No one said anything and that was hard for me."
"Everyone treated me different, and I didn't like that."

"I couldn't concentrate for the longest time."

"It was fine going back. My friends helped a lot."

"I felt like I had a big sign on that said I was different."

"Kids made fun of me behind my back and sometimes to my face."

Many schools have become better equipped and educated in dealing positively with children who experience a death. But many still have a long way to go. When I was in the sixth grade in Pennsylvania in the sixties, I had a friend named Sandy whose mother was dying of breast cancer. Although we hung out together frequently, sometimes at her house, where we had to be quiet because of her mother's illness, I don't remember our ever directly talking about it. We didn't have the language to. I also think we believed if we didn't talk about it, maybe it wasn't really happening. I remember passing hours in fantasy play on the grounds of the school where Sandy's father was a caretaker. While we played as children often do, carelessly and unconscious of time, there was an edge of dare and risk taking to our play, an almost desperate quality of testing the limits. I believe now it was our way of playing out resistance to the fate that faced Sandy.

When her mother died, the news was delivered dispassionately by our sixth-grade teacher in Sandy's absence. No one asked a question. "When Sandy returns to school in a couple of days," we were instructed, "don't look at her funny." That was the extent of public processing. I don't know what any of the other students said to Sandy when she returned, if anything, but as one of her closest friends I said pitifully little, perhaps a mumbled, "Sorry about your mother." I didn't know what else to say. There was no guidance from any adults around us.

Kids at The Dougy Center, especially from middle school ages up, talk a lot about how their friendships were strengthened or lost following their parent's death. Almost all of them talk about feeling different and wanting to be treated the same. What was it like for you? How did your friends respond to your parent's death and was it helpful or harmful for you?

In closing, I want to reiterate that how others responded to you following your parent's death did not *determine* but did *influence* you. We are all shaped by those around us and the consequences of our choices. Understanding those influences, and looking honestly and non-judgmentally at ourselves can help us decide whether we're living the life we want to live or whether we've let outside circumstances disproportionately influence who we are as adults. In the following chapter, we'll explore how your age and developmental tasks influenced the person you have become.

My Notes

My Notes

_____
_____
_____
_____
_____
_____
_____
_____
_____
_____
_____
_____
_____
_____
_____
_____
_____
_____
_____
_____
_____

CHAPTER
FIVE

What Kind of Kid
Were You?

How Old Were You When
Your Parent Died?

Your age when your parent died makes a difference in
how you understood and reacted to the loss at the time.
What's more important, however, than your *chronological*
age is your *developmental* age, which is trickier to define.
For example, while we may say that most children will
begin to walk at a certain age, the reality is that there's a
range of time during which most children will begin to
walk, and we can't conclusively say exactly when a specific
child will do so. However, a child who's walking at six

97

months would be considered extremely unusual, and one not walking by three years would be cause for concern.

As we take a look at some stages of children's development and the approximate age ranges for these stages, remember they are flexible and provide a way of looking at how children mature. The most important aspect here is exploring what normal tasks and challenges faced you before you even had to deal with the reality of your parent's death and the loss that entailed. It may be that coping with your parent's death interrupted your growing-up tasks or, at the very least, provided an additional hurdle. Consider that possibility and remember—without judgment!—as you read about yourself below.

We'll look at four ranges of childhood and some of the usual expectations for these age ranges. I'm using a slightly adjusted pairing of two respected theories about childhood development, those of American psychologist Erik Erikson and Swiss psychologist Jean Piaget. Erikson theorized about how children develop psychosocially, that is, in relationship to others. Piaget's interest in cognitive development focused more on the child's intellect and understanding, his or her internal makeup. I'm collapsing Erikson's original five stages into four for ease of discussion, and slightly adjusting the chronological age ranges of each to correspond with four periods, but the essence of their theories remains.

The issue we really want to look at is this: Your parent's death when you were a baby, preschooler, preadolescent, or teenager threw an unexpected monkey wrench into your growing-up challenges. What were those challenges, even before the death happened? And how might those challenges have become even bigger challenges after your parent's death?

Birth to Two: Infants and Babies/Developing Trust

Here you are, new to the world, suddenly thrust from your comfortable close quarters into chaos and outsiders! Piaget called this stage of life the *sensorimotor* period. You were using your senses to experience the world and your body: seeing objects, shapes, and people; tasting milk and later other foods as they were fed to you; feeling both warmth and discomfort; hearing loud sounds, soothing sounds, and scary sounds; smelling substances that attracted or repelled you. You made sounds, but it was awhile before you could form words anyone else understood.

You began to experience patterns. When you cried, someone picked you up. When you got hungry, someone fed you. When you pooped, someone cleaned you up. You began to recognize certain people who usually did these things for you, and they started to feel safe. Or you weren't fed, held, or cleaned because of abuse or neglect and didn't experience safety. Either way, you were doing the same work of infancy—sensing and searching for patterns, as well as safety. As it turns out, this is a lifelong task, but as an infant, you were starting at the most elemental levels.

You also were beginning to recognize that your toes, fingers, and nose (among other body parts) were a part of you, as you began to sense that there was a *you,* and that other people and objects were *not you.* In relationship to these "not-yous," Erikson defined your primary task during this period as developing trust. If the patterns of others made your environment feel safe and secure, you carried a foundation of trust into the next phase of growth. If the patterns of others did not create safety, you carried mistrust and fear into the next phase. If the others around you were unpredictable, as is the norm for those raised in abusive homes, the patterns you were searching for were much harder to predict. You adapted to the pattern of unpredictability.

So what does this have to do with you if one or both of your parents died during your infancy?

If your parent died at your birth or shortly thereafter, it means that there was one less "not you" to assist in your building of patterns and trust, though others may have taken his or her place. It means that your surviving parent was under considerable stress, regardless of the quality of his or her caregiving. And it may mean that the early patterns you thought you had down were suddenly changed, both in terms of who those "others" were, and in what you had learned to predict. Because of the bond of birth mother and child, if your mother died, you intuitively, instinctually sensed the absence of that particular other, both in sheer physical absence (having spent nine months or so literally attached to her), and in the changes of those around you. In short, there very likely was an interruption in your ability to develop trust in your environment and the people in it. Whether and how that trust was generated or regained had a lot to do with what happened next in your family and world.

The Preschooler's Work: Declaring Selfhood and Taking Initiative

On whatever foundation of trust or mistrust you gained the first couple years of life, you headed into the next phase, which Piaget called the *preoperational* period, from roughly two to five or six years old. You started to realize things and people had names, and you began to develop a language for your world, another way of making sense of it. You developed both a boundless curiosity and an inventive need for autonomy, evidenced by common utterances of children this age: "What's that?" and "No!"

You saw yourself as the center of the universe, which everyone and everything revolved around, and in many ways your dependence on others reinforced this short-lived fantasy. In Erikson's model, your task during the early preoperational stage, roughly ages two and three, was to exercise your independence, while also experiencing some shame and doubt. Toilet training illustrates this tension, as you were encouraged and rewarded to leave diapers behind, and perhaps embarrassed (or ridiculed) when you didn't make it to the potty.

From roughly three to six, your language skills improved, you interacted with others your age, and you began the challenge of learning concepts like sharing and waiting your turn, as well as tasks like putting toys away and buttoning your coat. Erikson defined the developmental issues at this age as the struggle between taking initiative and feeling guilt. You were encouraged to do things on your own, but you also developed an awareness of having done things wrong, of responsibility for your actions or failure to act.

So how does this relate to your experience when your mother or father died? Even before the death, at this age your primary tasks were developing independence and initiative. At the very least, when your parent died, you were doubly challenged just as you were struggling with these formidable tasks. It's as if just as you began to walk, the rug was pulled out from under you. Your autonomy and the steps you had already taken to be a separate self were compromised. You may have slipped back to younger behaviors, a common consequence of a parent's death for preschool grievers. A lot of parents complain that their child seems to have lost ground, reverting to behaviors he or she had already outgrown, including baby talk, wetting the bed, clinging to people, crying more frequently, and insisting on their own way. The parenting challenge increases at the same time your surviving parent had less resources to draw on because of his or her own grief. And well-meaning others had all kinds of advice about what you should or should not be told, as well as whether, and at what level, to involve you in funeral services or end-of-life rituals.

At the same time, you were trying to understand what happened to your mother or father, and what you had to do with it. Although you had a sense of someone going away, or being gone, you didn't fully understand that death meant *forever,* that your parent was never coming back. Four-year-old Tobias, a week after his father's death, expressed that "I know you said Daddy's dead, but is he going to be dead all week?" Five-year-old Kathryn, who was struggling to understand where her mother was, was told by relatives that she had died and was in heaven. Because the family previous to the death shared no religious beliefs with her, "heaven" was no different to her than if they'd said "Wichita" or "Hoboken." To further complicate matters, they told her that God had wanted her mommy; and because she had no context for "God," she understandably was angry with God who had taken her mommy away from her. (Even children who have a context for God because of their religious upbringing frequently question why God allowed their parent to die.)

At this age children are repetitive. You wanted to read, or be read, the same stories, over and over. You asked the same questions again and again. This is part of the learning process, and it's also part of being validated by the "other." I remember watching a father and his three- or four-year-old son at an airport while I was waiting for a flight. As they stood looking out the window at arriving and departing planes, the boy exclaimed, "That's a big plane!" and looked at his father with delight. "Yes, that's a big plane!" his father validated, smiling and looking at his son. For over fifteen minutes they continued this verbal volley, barely varying their words. "That's a big BIG plane!" the child stated emphatically and looked expectantly at Dad. "That IS a big BIG plane!" Dad concurred, as his son squealed with delight. As the father mirrored the boy's words, I could literally see this boy fill with the pride and the empowering accomplishment of *simply being heard.* No doubt you've also witnessed the opposite of this sensitive and supportive interaction between parents and young children—the questioning child in the store whose arm is practically pulled from the socket as an exasperated parent tells him to shut up. It is through the patterns of these interactions that we begin to form impressions about the world and how we should respond to it *in order to be safe.* At this preoperational stage, one of the ways we do so is to ask the same questions over and over.

This trait may be particularly exasperating for the exhausted and stressed parent struggling with his or her spouse's death. You wanted to know what was happening. You wanted to know the story. But you may have learned that it was not okay to ask. Or that if you asked, your mom or dad would cry, go away, or get harsh with you. Because you were looking for patterns, and safety, you may have learned to keep quiet. Your surviving parent may have assumed you were too young to understand, or that if he or she "protected you" from the details, you would be better off. At The Dougy Center in our "Littles" groups for three-to-five-year olds, parents frequently inform us that their child doesn't really know or understand what happened. They assume that because the child isn't telling them what they think or have heard, that the child doesn't know anything. Children tend to "fill in the gaps" with their own story if they don't get the information they ask for. And they usually know much more than adults think they know.

You may or may not have been included in the discussions, decisions, or rituals following your parent's death. Did you attend a funeral? Did you see your parent's dead body? Or were you shuffled off to a baby-sitter or family member because you were "too young" to understand? (Do you even know?) Because of the common misconceptions that children are either too young to understand, too fragile to be exposed to death, or so resilient it won't matter, many families, unfortunately, do not involve or allow children's participation when a death occurs. It's as if in shielding them, we assume we're protecting them. Of the more than ten thousand children who have entered The Dougy Center's grief support groups, I have yet to hear one, of any age, say she is glad to have been shielded from the events and decisions around a parent's death. I've never heard a child say he was happy he wasn't allowed to go to the funeral; nor have I heard one say he was happy to be forced to attend. The key issue is choice—informed choice. But most adults don't understand what grieving children need or understand. In a well-intentioned effort to protect you, they may have excluded you. They didn't understand that you would feel this exclusion as a slight, as if what you felt or thought didn't matter. They didn't realize how much you needed to be included or at least have the option to choose whether and how you wanted to be included.

To complicate matters further for you as a grieving preschooler, you were just beginning to grapple with feelings like shame and guilt. Because of your belief that the world revolved around you, you may have thought that you somehow caused, or could have prevented, your parent's death. This "magical thinking" is part of a child's natural development at this age. It's believing that events happen because you made them happen. You may have thought you were responsible for your parent's death. And perhaps you thought that because you caused it, you could also "uncause" it, or bring your parent back. "If I was strong enough and big enough, I could fly over there and make my daddy be okay," four-year-old Bradley shared with the other kids in his "Littles" group at the center. The other children told their own stories of bravado and strength, as if to combat what adults told them. Kids of this age reveal their struggles, frustrations, and hope in their play. In a very real sense, play is their work. At The Dougy Center, through sand-tray play, dress-up clothes, puppets, art, games, and toys, children show us through their play what their words often cannot capture:

Four-year-old Derrick, slapping and shouting at a teddy bear, "Bad bear! Bad bear! You killed my daddy!"

LeShane, five, setting up a cemetery scene in the sand tray, complete with skeletons and buried caskets, grave markers, and people around the edges, who, he says, are crying. Suddenly, his eyes brighten and he instructs, "Watch!" Digging the caskets out, releasing the skeletons, he smiles slyly and says, "I'm going to make them okay again!"

Jessica, three, whose father died after rescue workers tried fruitlessly to save his life after a heart attack in their living room. Taking control in the dress-up room, she dons a play stethoscope and makes "all better" a doll that's lying still on the ground.

Derrick, LeShane, and Jessica were attempting to make

sense of the new world their parent's death had placed them in. But they were also, in keeping with their developmental tasks of independence and initiative, trying to exert control over an event they were unable to prevent and may even believe they contributed to. Formidable tasks for three, four, five, and six year olds. Formidable tasks for you at that age.

The Preadolescent Challenge: Getting to Work and Confronting Inferiority

As a six to eleven or twelve year old, you started school, had increasing interaction with others your age, and began what Erikson's model calls the stage of "industry versus inferiority." Industry refers to devoting oneself to tasks, and at this age, there are many: reading, writing, math, and all kinds of new challenges. Piaget called this time "concrete operations," where an understanding of symbols, logical thinking, and organizational skills develop. During this time, you are encouraged and/or discouraged by those around you: other children, teachers, friends, and family. You start to gain aptitude for certain skills, perhaps math or language. You are seeking cues from others for reinforcement, and you begin to compare yourself to others. You were told you were good at math, so you probably enjoyed math. If you were slower to read, you may have wanted to avoid reading so as not to look stupid. You thrived, or failed to thrive, on the responses of others. This is not to imply that who we become is totally dependent on others, but our lives begin to be shaped by those who encourage us, and by those who fail to encourage us.

If your parent died before this age, you know that you were already doubly challenged in your tasks of developing trust, independence, and initiative. Now you can add industry to the list. If your parent died when you were between six and twelve, your growth interruption occurred in the area of industry, that is, during the time you were learning new tasks and comparing yourself to others. Many of the kids we've worked with of this age at The Dougy Center who've had a parent die experience a kind of temporary, though significant, paralysis in their development. Some talk about difficulty concentrating or focusing. Others regress to younger behaviors. Many report somatic symptoms: difficulty sleeping, headaches, problems eating. Children with stable, caring support are better able to develop competency in their industry efforts than those whose self-concepts are challenged by a lack of reinforcement. This doesn't mean the latter are fated to fail; it simply means they have more challenges to overcome in order to succeed.

During this developmental period, most children do understand death as final. But they often retain the belief that in some way their actions, or failure to act, may have contributed to a death. Here are a few examples:

Eleven-year-old Jackie's father died in a shoot-out with the police. She thought it was her fault he died because "he worried about me and stuff."

David, ten, whose father died of a cocaine overdose, said that if only he'd asked his father to pick him up after school that day, he could have saved him.

Bettina, nine, whose mother died in a car accident, was convinced that her mother died because that morning Bettina had "stolen" her mother's favorite scarf. If she hadn't, she believed, she wouldn't have been punished by having her mother die.

As adults it's easy to look at such examples and know that in no way did these children cause or contribute to their parents' deaths. But simply telling them so doesn't necessarily change their beliefs. What about you? Think back to the circumstances of your parent's death. Was there something you thought you should have done, or could have done, that would have spared his or her life? It doesn't matter whether the logical, mature twenty-five, thirty-five, forty-five, or fifty-five year old knows it wasn't so. You may still be carrying that seven year old or twelve year old's memories and beliefs. If so, we'll look at what to do with that later in the book. For now, just be aware whether this was something you told yourself or not. Later we'll also look at other emotions and their legacies, and what you can do with them.

Raging Adolescence: Developing Identity in a Confusing Time

It's amusing how once we're adults we look at adolescents as a foreign species, even though we all went through those challenging teen years ourselves. As young people enter the teen years, they embark on establishing an identity, often by testing out what fits and what doesn't, primarily against the crucible of peer opinion, informed to some degree by internalized values. Sometimes values get pushed aside in the fire of peer pressure. During the teen years hormonal changes and adaptations, as well as the increasing desire for independence, can make for challenging decision making.

Piaget's model describes a move from concrete operational to "formal operational," into a more complex realm of abstract thoughts and ideas, higher level questioning about meaning and life, and more advanced reasoning. At a time when you were already questioning everything, your parent died. The search to understand why, and why *you,* was paramount. Adults may not have been particularly helpful in your search for answers. Many teens tell us at The Dougy Center they're encouraged to "get over it," "go on," and "put this behind" them, most often from teachers, coaches, or other adults who are disappointed with late papers, a lack of concentration and focus, or other behaviors. Your need to find or make meaning from your

111

parent's death may be a lifelong process, particularly if that need was not supported through the words or actions of those around you.

Erikson defines the tasks in this developmental period as "identity versus role confusion," as the teen struggles to leave dependency behind and establish independence and adulthood. You can see where your parent's death may have altered the course of this task for you. You may have been forced, through this life experience, to "grow up" quicker than you might otherwise have needed to. Your independence, so avidly craved, may not have been the welcome treat you thought it would be.

As you may recall, the middle school and high school years are characterized by intense peer pressure, questioning about meaning and one's place and role in life, and the increasing need for separation from one's parents. It's a time of cliques and factions, of those who are "in" and those who are "out," of finding a place to fit in (even if that place is *not* fitting in). If your parent died when you were a teenager, this event made you different from your friends and peers at a time when being different hurts. You may have experienced added pressures and responsibilities, as well as financial concerns or questions about your future. If you had a conflicted relationship with your parent who died, as many teens do, you may have carried the additional weight and burden of guilt or unresolved issues. Do any of these experiences ring true for you?

Grief Gets Reprocessed Throughout Life

The nature of loss and grieving, contrary to popular belief that it gets "resolved" or that it ends, is that you continually reprocess loss during each phase of your life. From childhood through adolescence and into adulthood, you were constantly reminded of the loss of your parent, on holidays like Mother's Day or Father's Day, at times of celebration like graduations, as well as in the simple everyday ups and downs of your life. You had to confront the reality of not having that parent in your life while coping with new challenges—friends, relationships, dating, career choices, whether to marry and have children. You didn't have your parent around to help you with decisions or share your joys and problems. Even as an adult, each time you faced a pivotal point in your life, you probably were reminded of your parent's absence. "My father didn't get to see me graduate from high school," seventeen-year-old Sonya lamented in a group at The Dougy Center. "And he won't be around to give me away if I get married, and he'll never get to be a grandfather. My kids will never have that grandfather, and that makes me really sad." Other kids had two parents, and there were constant reminders that you didn't. Your triumphs in life have probably been tempered a bit as you reflected on wishing your father or mother could have been around to celebrate with you. The death of your parent truly changed your life, forever.

★   ★   ★

We've looked here at some general developmental issues that influenced you at the time of your parent's death. What theories like Piaget's and Erikson's don't focus on as much are the unique elements of your personality, your social and cognitive abilities, your temperament and style of thinking and processing and how those affected your experience. What else do we know about resiliency, the ability to recover from difficult circumstances, and how does that information apply to you? We'll take a look at this in the next chapter.

My Notes

_____

_____

_____

_____

_____

_____

_____

_____

_____

_____

_____

_____

_____

_____

_____

_____

_____

_____

_____

My Notes

_____

_____

_____

_____

_____

_____

_____

_____

_____

_____

_____

_____

_____

_____

_____

_____

_____

_____

_____

_____

_____

_____

What We Know About Children and Resiliency: The Good, the Bad, and the Ugly

If you listen to talk-show hosts, read self-help books, or follow conventional wisdom, you'll find all kinds of advice about how to overcome just about any setback: depression, low self-esteem, a bad marriage. In our post-Freud era replete with hundreds, if not thousands of therapeutic solutions and modalities, never has there been such an emphasis on personal growth and healing. And yet the numbers of people suffering from depression continues to skyrocket. The highest category of disability insurance claims filed are stress related. We spout sayings like "It takes a village to raise a child" and "It's never too late to have a happy childhood," but how much do we really know (let alone practice!) about what it takes to raise a child into healthy adulthood?

Well, there's good news and bad news.

The good news is we know a lot.

The bad news is, at least for you and me, we can't go back, reeducate our relatives and other influential adults, and relive our childhoods with these things in mind. But we can do a better job of raising our own children and positively influencing the many "at risk" children who will pass through our lives. And I believe having a clearer understanding of how you survived will help you more fully live the life you were meant to live, using your skills and talents and uniqueness to make the world a better place. A lofty goal? Yes, but consider the alternatives. I think Thoreau's reflections at Walden Pond remain true today: "Most men [and women, I'd add] live lives of quiet desperation." Why? Because we haven't grasped and put into practice what is known about how to live a life of fulfillment.

In this chapter, we're going to look at what we know, and what we think we know, about how children who are considered "at risk" succeed in life. I would include you in that category because you had a parent die. (On a more philosophical level, I'd maintain that we all enter the world "at risk.") You've probably wondered at some point in your life why you've made it to where you have, and why some others didn't. We've already explored some of the factors that influenced you as a child, including the losses and changes you experienced, how others influenced you, and how age-related tasks may have affected your development. Now we'll look at what we know about resilience, especially in children.

Let's look at the word *resilience*. It derives from the Latin word *resilire,* meaning "to leap back." We think of resilience as the ability to recover from difficult circumstances, to be buoyant. I also like a secondary interpretation of the word from *The American Heritage Dictionary:* "The property of a material that enables it to resume its original shape or position after being bent, stretched, or compressed." Your parent's death bent, stretched, or compressed you. How did you bounce back?

There's a question I'd like you to be thinking about as you read through this chapter. It may be one you haven't given much thought. Frequently we focus on what's going wrong or what's gone wrong in our lives. Let's flip to the other side. As we explore the creative ways that children bounce back from difficult situations, and you apply it to yourself, ask yourself: *What went right?* What did you do, and what did others do, to help you be the person you are today? You may be both surprised by and proud of your ability to bounce back.

Resiliency studies and research about what helps kids "bounce back" are subject to the same kinds of potential pitfalls in research findings we looked at earlier. How can we *truly* pinpoint the factors that helped Christopher become a successful businessman and father, while Charlotte, raised in the same family, has struggled with alcohol addiction and can't hold a job?

Among many resiliency studies is one conducted by Werner and Smith[1] which has followed 698 individuals from the womb up through several decades of their lives. The Kauai Longitudinal Study collected a barrage of data on them prebirth, between their births in 1955, and at age two, ten, eighteen, and thirty or thirty-one. Their findings refer to three "protective factors" that seemed to separate those who bounced back from those who didn't. This is just one study, but others have come to essentially similar conclusions. As we look at these three factors, think about how they apply to you. In your case, *what went right?*

Factor 1: Your Internal Makeup

Werner and Smith noted that resilient children had at least average intelligence, but to me the most interesting part about resilient children's internal makeup is that they had traits or attributes that elicited positive responses from family members and strangers. In other words, those who bounced back were basically *likeable kids!* Another researcher, Garmezy,[2] noted that resilient children were rated by adults as friendly, cooperative, emotionally stable, and well-liked by peers. Again, adults liked them *because they were likeable.* They had a positive sense of self, and an internal locus of control. They figured out how to develop social skills that attracted people to them. They were born with and/or developed attributes and traits that pulled people in rather than pushed them away. I don't think we can ever fully prove which comes first, positive responses or positive traits. But it's not difficult to see that they tend to reinforce one another, contributing to constructive or destructive cycles and patterns.

Emerging from Werner and Smiths' findings were specific personality traits or personality predispositions in resilient children. This begs the inherently unanswerable question of nature versus nurture: Are resilient kids *born resilient,* or do they *develop resilience* because their positive efforts to get their needs met are reinforced by others? Most research supports a combination of the two. According to the study, resilient children displayed the following five characteristics: They were affectionate; had easy-going temperaments; good reasoning skills; positive self-esteem; and an internal locus of control, "a strong belief that they could control their fates by their own actions."[3] As K. Butler extrapolated on Werner and Smiths' findings in an article on resilience: "By the time they were in high school . . . the resilient children were significantly more likely than nonresilient children to have an 'inner locus of control'—an optimistic confidence in their ability to shape events. In other words, they had developed both competence and hope."[4]

I'm assuming if you've read this far you would consider

yourself above average in intelligence. You can probably also pat yourself on the back for your ability to attract people to yourself. But, as Butler points out, "resilient people do not make it on inborn strengths, fierce independence and rugged individualism alone."[5] You found some other people to help you.

Factor 2: Your Immediate Family

The second protective factor Werner and Smith identified in resilient children they refer to as affectional ties with parents or parent substitutes, such as grandparents or older siblings. These relationships encouraged trust, autonomy, and initiative. Garmezy spoke of this as emotional support within the family, or, if no such biological adult relationship existed, having at least one significant positive adult relationship.

Previously we explored the influence of your surviving parent and your family environment through the lens of your parent's death. Although most of the resiliency literature is not specific to coping with parental death, it is nevertheless relevant to a cross section of risk factors. Various researchers have explored protective factors within families that encourage bouncing back. Here are ten family resiliency factors that played a role in your life. As you read these, check off which of these statements were characteristic of your family more often than not.[6] (Keeping in mind that no family displays any of these characteristics all of the time in every circumstance. Check off what was *generally* true of your immediate family after your parent died.):

1. _____ Our communication patterns were affirming, caring, and supportive.
2. _____ We valued self-reliance and independence and an equal respect for each family member.
3. _____ We had some kind of spiritual belief and practices that acknowledged reason and logic alone couldn't explain what had happened to us.
4. _____ We had flexibility in our roles, rules, and lifestyles.
5. _____ We valued, practiced, and searched for truthfulness.
6. _____ We were able to maintain hope for the future.
7. _____ We had a commitment to work together, and a sense of control and influence over the challenges we faced.
8. _____ We maintained some family routines and family time.
9. _____ We had social support outside of our family.
10. _____ Our family was essentially physically and emotionally healthy.

You'll note some familiar themes here: truth, commitment, hope, optimism, flexibility, a sense of control, a sense of meaning. If you were fortunate enough to grow up in a family where these traits were valued and practiced, you probably were very resilient. If these were not characteristic of your family, and you bounced back anyway, chances are you found others to fulfill these roles for you. Because no one, and no family, grows in a vacuum.

Factor 3: Your External Support System

Werner and Smiths' third factor influencing resilient children found they had external support systems in youth groups, school, or religious communities that rewarded their competence and provided them with a sense of coherence and grounding. A thread through almost all of the resiliency literature finds that one caring adult (or a succession of them) makes a difference.

After your parent died, who was there for you?

As Butler noted, "Those most adept at recruiting surrogate caregivers and adult mentors are the ones who eventually are the most resilient and self-reliant."[7] The key word here is "recruiting." In other words, these people who cared about you didn't just happen along. Consider the possibility that you were the active agent of your success. You can be grateful that specific people happened by at the time they did, but you made them look your way. What would you have done if so-and-so hadn't come along? You'd have found someone else to come along with you!

Wolin and Wolin, in their excellent book, *The Resilient Self: How Survivors of Troubled Families Rise Above Diversity,*[8] point out that while the importance of mentors, surrogate parents, or significant adults in the lives of resilient children cannot be overlooked, what is often underemphasized is the role of the child in these relationships. They reframe what's frequently construed as "the Save-the-Child Drama" to "the Appealing Child Meets the Potentially Interested Adult."[9] Resilient children aren't just passive flowers waiting by the wayside for some bystander to notice. They are exhibiting behaviors to get people interested in them. Sometimes these behaviors are referred to by adults as "acting out." Of course they are! All children "act out" their need for nurture, love, and support. They may act it out in ways adults like and that encourage reinforcement. Or they may act it out in ways adults don't like, which encourages alienation. Resilient children develop the combination of traits that attract people to them.

How did you cope as a child? How did you "act out" your needs? All behavior is purposeful; all behavior is a way of trying to stay safe in the world. You were strategic, and you learned how to take care of yourself. The strategies you employed were ingenious at the time and enabled you to survive. The question now is, in what ways are those same strategies still working—or not working—for you?

Resiliency After the Death of a Parent

With this background information about the traits of resilient children, let's take a look at what resiliency studies specific to parentally bereaved children add to our understanding. Is there anything we can add that might help provide additional insight on factors that contributed to your resilience?

Three behaviors characteristic of resilient parentally bereaved children emerged from the literature. Remember that these findings don't *prove* anything; rather, they lend credence to educated guesses based on research and experience. Here are the three behaviors specific to the resilience of children grieving the death of a parent:

Behavior 1: Children Who Maintain Psychological Connections with Their Deceased Parent Are More Likely to Make Better Long-Term Adjustments Than Those Who Do Not[10]

Literature on resilient bereaved children as well as healthy grieving supports the idea of maintaining connection with the deceased parent. This is not generally understood or reinforced in mainstream American culture as children and adults are encouraged to "move on" and "put this behind you." Our society feeds on fast solutions and happy endings, and the process of grieving the loss of a parent is lifelong. Psychological connections with the deceased parent may take many forms. Check off any that you remember doing as a child or adolescent:

_____ I wore jewelry or clothing that belonged to my parent.

_____ I had some of his or her belongings in my possession.

_____ I got my parent's ashes or visited the grave site.

_____ I talked and reminisced with others about my parent.

_____ I wrote letters to him or her.

_____ I spoke to his or her picture or their image in my mind.

_____ I made a memory book to capture stories, photos, and other memories.

You may or may not have received encouragement from your surviving parent, other family members, friends, or community to maintain psychological connections with your deceased parent, but "the evidence is that some children persist in the activities of resilience despite discouragement and barriers."[11]

Behavior 2: Adolescents Who Are Able to Successfully Maintain a Changing Mental Relationship with Their Deceased Parent Are More Likely to Be Resilient[12]

Your parent's death was a kind of freeze frame in time. You may wonder about what your deceased parent might be like if he or she had lived, or what kind of relationship you'd have now. But that part can only be played out in your imagination. You, however, continued to grow, age, and hopefully mature after your parent's death. Although it's a common response to idealize, or at least be kind about, the dead, a key part of adolescence is separating, or deidealizing one's parents. "Adolescents who are able to successfully maintain a changing mental relationship with their deceased parent—one that is not a static representation of their relationship at the time of the parent's death— are more likely to be resilient."[13] In other words, although your parent was no longer able to change, your understanding of your parent as you received new information or insight, provided the opportunity for a dynamic, rather than a static, psychological relationship.

Behavior 3: Healthy Grieving Involves Both Avoidance and Reminiscence in a Balancing Interplay[14]

Denial often gets a bad rap in psychology, but it actually is both necessary and potentially healing when balanced with expression. That expression may take many different forms. Not everyone cries, or needs to. Not everyone talks, or needs to. But I do believe everyone needs to find their own methods of expression and understanding, and that if they don't, their grief will still be pounding at the doors of their soul demanding exit. Horowitz, Marmar, Weiss, DeWitt, and Rosenbaum highlighted the need for balance eloquently in their article, "Brief Psychotherapy of Bereavement Reactions," from which I quote:

> A healthy grieving pattern is one in which the bereaved uses both avoidance and purposive reminiscence, whereas heavy reliance on either one to the exclusion of the other is an unhealthy pattern . . . individuals should not remain at the beck and call of all their grief experiences without relief; hence intermittent periods of avoidance are in the service of healthy bereavement. Likewise, excessive avoidance leads to a failure to develop the necessary ability to tolerate the sadness and anguish associated with the death, failure to confront the changed re-

alities of one's life situation, and failure to reorganize one's life in acknowledgment of the loss.[15]

So it isn't an either/or. Either you're in denial or you're emoting all the time. The healthier path is some of both.

Why Bereaved Children Are at High Risk

In closing the discussion on what we know about children at risk and protective factors that contribute to resilience, I'd like to revisit the "significant seven" characteristics research studies have shown are more prevalent in parentally bereaved children than in their nonbereaved counterparts. The relevance of these characteristics is highlighted when they're juxtaposed with what we know about characteristics of resilient children and illustrate why I believe bereaved children are at high risk, particularly of carrying these seven characteristics into adulthood. If you take a look at this comparison chart, it will become clear.

A COMPARISON OF CHARACTERISTICS OF BEREAVED CHILDREN AND RESILIENT CHILDREN

The Significant Seven Characteristics of Bereaved Children	*Five Personality Traits or Predispositions of Resilient Children*
External locus of control	Internal locus of control
Lower self-esteem	Healthy self-esteem

The Significant Seven Characteristics of Bereaved Children	*Five Personality Traits or Predispositions of Resilient Children*
Higher levels of anxiety/ fearfulness	Easy-going temperament
Higher evidence of depression	Affectionate
More accidents and health problems	Good reasoning skills
Pessimism about the future	
Underperforming	

I believe the key at-risk factor bereaved children demonstrate in greater proportion than their nonbereaved peers is an external locus of control. Resilient children have a strong belief that they can control their fates by their own actions; bereaved children show a higher evidence of externalizing control, believing that their fate is in someone else's hands. No wonder they display higher levels of anxiety, depression, pessimism, health problems, underperformance, and lower self-esteem. We've looked in this chapter at characteristics, traits, and behaviors of resilient children, and you've had the opportunity to see how and where your resilience came from. Now, let's see what happened as you left your childhood behind. What did you carry into adulthood, and how has it served you?

My Notes

How Your Parent's Death in Childhood Affects You Now

Today I received an email from a woman who said she "stumbled upon" The Dougy Center's Web site, and found herself "hungry for some information about me. You see," she wrote, "I am a grieving child locked in the body of a grown woman. My mother was killed suddenly days before my third birthday. My father was in Vietnam at the time, and my care was given by well-meaning family members. However, I wasn't allowed to attend any of the services held for my mother. To make things worse, because my parents were so young at the time—early twenties—no one spoke of my mother for fear of upsetting my new 'mother.' I am now a thirty-three-year-old woman who struggles with grief issues daily. I have gone on with life on the outside and been successful in everyone's eyes . . . but only my husband knows the real pain I carry deep inside."

Sharon is not the only "grieving child locked in the body of a grown woman" or man. My guess is, if you were honest and could allow yourself to be vulnerable enough, you'd sense that grieving child within yourself, the child in you that still hurts. (If you find yourself automatically responding with "No, not me!" recognize how powerfully your need to stay safe, in control, and protected operates for you. That's what's helped you be resilient! It also may keep you stuck in some patterns that don't serve you well now.)

Up to this point we've looked at how your parent's death affected you as a child and teenager. We found evidence that as a parentally bereaved youth, you had a higher potential for seven symptoms than your nonbereaved peers.

Your Seven Risk Factors

1. Your chances of experiencing depression were higher.
2. You were susceptible to an increase in health problems and accidents.
3. You were more likely to believe that you were underperforming in your life.
4. You were prone to greater anxiety.

5. The odds that you suffer from lower self-esteem were higher.

6. You had a higher probability of believing that events in your life are a result of fate, luck, or other factors beyond your control (an external locus of control) versus a belief that you are in control of your own life (an internal locus of control).

7. You were at greater risk for envisioning the future with less optimism.

We looked at the developmental issues you faced at the time of your parent's death and beyond, and how the special circumstances of the death may have affected you. We saw the important influence of your surviving parent or adult caregivers, as well as other adults, and your wider community. And finally, we reviewed findings about resilient children, and the protective factors that help them bounce back from difficult circumstances or tragedies. What Now?

Now it's time to look at yourself in the present, as an adult who was parentally bereaved as a child. How does your parent's death in your childhood affect you *now?*

We're going to take a look at what we know about this topic from studies that have been conducted, and you'll have the opportunity to explore how your experience matches or strays from the research findings. As we do, we'll look at what appears at first to be a simple question:

How did this event in your childhood influence who you are now? The answer, as we will see, is not so simple.

What evidence is there that your parent's death has a relationship to how you are as an adult? You'll note that I've used the terminology "has a relationship to" rather than "causes." It's scientifically impossible to prove that the events in your childhood *caused* your behaviors in adulthood, for a couple of reasons. First, your parent's death was not the only event you've experienced that contributed to who you are today. It was a pivotal one, no doubt, but since we can't isolate that experience from all of the rest of your experiences, we can't conclusively *prove* that it is the sole root of who you are as an adult. Second, and perhaps more important, to claim that childhood events *determine* how we'll turn out as adults does not factor in the very important role of choice.

Having stated these "disclaimers," let's not rule out the importance of what we can't scientifically pin down or prove. I think we can clearly say that the events of childhood influence us. They do not, however (even when it feels like it), *control* us—unless we allow them to.

Most of the research on the long-term consequences of a parent's death in childhood looks at the topic in terms of psychopathology. That is, researchers want to know if parental death in childhood leads to clinically diagnosable mental or behavioral disorders in adulthood, the only kinds of mental health issues most insurance companies will provide coverage for. There are many claims, but the scientific evidence for an association between parental death and later psychopathology has been contradictory at best.

The limitations of research make it difficult to get reliable information. There are inherent problems in studying you now, as an adult, because we're usually using retrospective designs, which look back and try to guess what childhood events caused or contributed to which adult outcomes. Researchers would ask you, and other bereaved adults, lots of questions and give you tests, and then compare you to nonbereaved adults who responded to the same questions and tests. But this is a flawed process. Let's say we find that one hundred people who had a parent die in childhood eat twice as much chocolate as one hundred people who didn't have a parent die in childhood. Does this mean that having a parent die in childhood contributes to excessive consumption of chocolate? It might, but it might also be a fluke.

Another complication is that most often researchers use clinical or special populations, people who are hospitalized, seeking psychological help, in prison, or in some other special treatment circumstance, for their studies. Most of the studies in this area are looking for psychopathology, and most people—including you, I imagine—don't want to be referred to as psychopaths. The true origins of the word, however, are more revealing. *Psycho* from the Greek word *psukho,* means "soul." *Pathology,* from the Greek word *pathos,* means "suffering." So *psychopathology* literally means "soul suffering." In that respect, literally, all of us are psychopaths—we all have experienced soul suffering. It's just a question of degree!

For our purposes here, however, we're not going to address how your parent's death influences you now in terms of mental illness or clinical behavior disorders. Let's just look at some possible ways that the seven significant symptoms in children who are parentally bereaved might carry over into adulthood. Maybe you'll see two or three, or perhaps all seven, in yourself. Perhaps you'll see none, though I'd be surprised if that were the case.

In chapter 2, you responded to some questions as you reflected back on your childhood. Now, let's look at those same questions applied to your adult life—to you now.

Ask Yourself These Seven Questions:

1. Are you depressed, or do you experience depression more than you would like?
2. Have you had more than "your share" of illness, accidents, or health-related problems?
3. Do you believe that you are not living up to your potential or that you're never doing enough?

4. Do you experience anxiety and fear about your future?

5. Do you generally feel lower self-esteem than you'd like?

6. Do you believe that the events of your life are mostly random, fate, luck, and beyond your control?

7. Do you feel pessimistic and hopeless about the future?

If you answered yes to any of these questions, you're not unusual. Read on and remember that the strategies you developed to cope as a child after the death of your parent were ones that helped you survive. Some of those strategies have helped you succeed as an adult and some may be holding you back from who you truly want to be. Either way, try not to judge yourself. Just take what fits for you and ignore what doesn't. At the same time, be aware that what we block out from our awareness has ways of getting our attention.

I believe that the way these "symptoms" play out in our lives as adults falls into three general categories: relationships, performance, and life satisfaction. If you want stronger, more life-affirming relationships, a better handle on setting and reaching your potential, and more satisfaction about your role in the world, read on. Remember that these seven issues—depression, health problems, feelings of inadequacy, anxiety, low self-esteem, helplessness, and pessimism are **symptoms.** They're trying to get your attention. Because they generally don't feel very good, we often respond by trying to avoid them. We attempt to keep the feelings away by self-medicating with alcohol and other drugs, staying busy, or a host of other avoidance behaviors. These symptoms are like inner kids who will keep adopting more and more outrageous behaviors until we open the door and see what they have to teach us.

1. *Are You Depressed, or Do You Experience Depression More Than You Would Like?*

The genetic roots of depression seem now to be beyond controversy. But I'm persuaded that an even more significant factor was the death of my mother when I was thirteen. This disorder and early sorrow—the death or disappearance of a parent, especially a mother, before or during puberty—appears repeatedly in the literature on depression as a trauma sometimes likely to create nearly irreparable emotional havoc. The danger is especially apparent if the young person is affected by what has been termed "incomplete mourning"—has, in effect, been unable to achieve the catharsis of grief, and so carries within himself through later years an insufferable burden of which rage and guilt, and not only dammed-up sorrow, are a part, and become the potential seeds of self-destruction.[1]

William Styron, the successful author of *Sophie's Choice,* among other novels, was in his sixties and suicidal before he realized he'd been depressed for most of his life. As he courageously explored the origins and reasons for his depression, he made a connection between his mother's death when he was thirteen and his failure to mourn as he needed to over the ensuing years. As I looked at what the research says about adult depression and childhood bereavement, I found that depression was the most commonly cited long-term consequence of parental death. However, consider the following two statements, both published the same year in credible professional publications:

"Parental bereavement during childhood increases the risk of depression in adulthood by a factor of about two or three."[2]

"There is no sound base of empirical data to support the theorized relationship between parental death during childhood and adult depression or any subtype of adult depression."[3]

Of the numerous professional articles claiming to show a relationship between adult depression and childhood parental bereavement, four stood out:

1,250 adults filled out a questionnaire and depression scale at their physician's office. Those who had experienced the death of a parent during childhood reported a significantly higher level of depression as adults.[4]

In a study of the impact of a parent's death in childhood on women's later role as mothers, researchers compared twenty-eight mothers of at least one child under age ten who had experienced the death of a parent before age thirteen to a control group of mothers who didn't have a parent die. They found that the bereaved women had significantly higher levels of depression and suicidality.[5]

Ninety-eight adults admitted to the emergency room after attempting suicide were matched to 102 adults by age and gender from a general practice. They found that those who had attempted suicide had a significantly higher incidence of bereavement during childhood than the comparison group.[6]

Sixty women who had been diagnosed with major depression were compared to four hundred nondepressed women, and the study found that there were no significant differences in the rate of childhood bereavement between the depressed and the comparison group.[7]

So the studies reveal conflicting results. What are we to believe?

I recommend that you trust your own experience. Let's say you recognize that you've experienced a lot of depression as an adult. The logical question you might ask is: Am

I depressed because of the death of my mother or father and my "dammed-up sorrow"?

The possible answers are:

1. Yes.
2. No.
3. Maybe.
4. Maybe partly, but that's not the only reason.

It's pretty hard to answer this question definitively because most often depression is not simply the result of one experience, event, or circumstance. Your depression may be related to a series of bad relationships you've been in over the years or your inability to hold a job. Those events may or may not be related to how you processed your parent's death. Other losses and disappointments may have added fuel to the fire of depression. Or you may be one of those people who is biologically predisposed to depression because of your genetic makeup.

But the key question to ask yourself is this: Have I mourned the death of my parent and how that loss changed my life, or do I have the sense that there's more to it?

If you sense there's "unaddressed business," it's not too late. Don't be misled, however, by the term "incomplete mourning," which, almost by definition implies there's such a thing as "complete mourning." There's no magical moment in grieving where you can say it's over and done with. There's no final finish line to cross. Because you are never the same, mourning is a lifelong process. What you can do, however, if you choose, is to face what's incomplete *for you* and do something about it. And believe it or not, there is good news about depression. We'll look at this further in the next chapter.

Now, on to question two:

2. Have You Had a High Number of Health Problems and Accidents?

As I write, I am waiting for a call from my family on the status of my father, who is three thousand miles away in his twenty-second day in an intensive care unit. I spent last week at what we thought was his deathbed, and returned to Portland after he seemed to rally. Yesterday morning my mother called to say he was failing, and the doctor had said at 9:00 A.M. that he'd die within the hour. Thirty hours later he's still breathing, and I'm waiting for "the call."

In these last twenty-four hours, I've slammed my finger in a hallway door, cut my thumb with a kitchen knife preparing dinner, and caught my wrist in the prongs of a three-ring binder hard enough to draw blood. It's not uncommon in times of high stress for us to experience a greater susceptibility to accidents, as well as illnesses, as our concentration and resistance is diminished. The link between depression and lowered immune functioning—

which helps us ward off colds, viruses, and bacteria—is well documented in medical studies.

I believe the same phenomenon happens when we repress or push out of our consciousness feelings that we'd rather not experience. These aren't "bad" feelings, but feelings that tend to make us feel uncomfortable: anger, sadness, fear, frustration, confusion, rage, depression, futility. When we keep them stuffed in, they're still there, affecting and infecting us, whether we're aware of it or not.

Conversely, there are probably ways in which the experience of your parent's death made you stronger. Many adults who had a parent die in childhood believe they've developed more sensitivity to others, have a greater understanding and appreciation of life and experience deeper relationships, knowing how abruptly they can end.

If you've experienced more than your share of illness or accidents, there may be a link between your unexpressed emotions and your susceptibility.

3. Do You Believe That You Are Not Living Up to Your Potential, or That You're Never Doing Enough?

Former Spice Girl Geri Halliwell, whose father died six months before she became a Spice Girl, said, "I think that kind of drove me. I had enough pain to make me desperately ambitious."[8]

The concept of success came up frequently in the more than one hundred interviews I conducted for this book with adults who had had a parent die in childhood. They tended to fall into two categories: those who expressed they didn't feel like they'd lived up to their potential (about 40 percent), and those who felt "driven" to succeed. More than 90 percent believed they had "grown up faster" than their nonbereaved counterparts. But even those who felt they'd been successful in large part due to the extra responsibilities they had to take on as children or teens indicated a sense that no matter what they did, it didn't seem to be enough.

I couldn't find many research studies that addressed this particular issue, though in the Butler study of mothers mentioned previously, those who'd had a parent die in childhood pushed harder to be perfect than nonbereaved mothers.[9] And indeed, there are highly successful adults in every field who lost a parent as a child. Consider this partial list of actors and performers, which reads like a celebrity success list: Tim Allen, Richard Belzer, Cate Blanchett, Dabney Coleman, Billy Crystal, Dan Day-Lewis, Gloria Estefan, Jane Fonda, Aretha Franklin, Fred Gandy, Sean Lennon, Joan Lunden, Bill Murray, Rosie O'Donnell, Cokie Roberts, Julia Roberts, Martin Sheen, and Barbara Streisand.

So there's nothing in the literature or real life to indicate that children and teens who lose a parent in childhood are destined to underperform. There is some evidence, however, that at least some feel driven to succeed. The question I'd invite you to consider is this: Can you recognize and celebrate what you have accomplished in your life? It may well be that you're not underperforming, but rather, underappreciating what you have done.

4. *Do You Experience Anxiety and Fear About Your Future?*

Among the research addressing anxiety and parental loss in childhood, consider the following:

The study of mothers who'd had a parent die in childhood found that bereaved mothers were significantly more worried about their own death and more overprotective with their children than nonbereaved mothers.

In a study of 1,018 pairs of adult female twins, 62 of the pairs had experienced the death of a parent before age seventeen. The bereaved twins had an increased risk for panic disorder and phobias.[10]

Although it's hard to *prove* a relationship between anxiety in adulthood and childhood loss of a parent, it makes a lot of sense that there could be a connection. If your parent died from a disease, you may have anxiety about whether you too might succumb to this disease. All of the adults I spoke with referred in some way to such a fear, especially if their parent died from a heart attack, breast

147

cancer, or other form of cancers known to have a genetic link. Many spoke of concerns when they approached the age their parent was when he or she died.

If your parent was murdered, suicided, or killed in an accident, you learned at an early age that the world was not always a safe place, that people you care about can die. You also had a heightened awareness of your own death. That's a lot for a child or teen to carry!

If you were raised in a destructive environment, or raised yourself, your anxiety and fear may have been well-founded, with deep roots.

There are various ways this anxiety may play out in your life now. Some, like forty-two-year-old Christina, report feeling caught in a dilemma: "On one hand," she said, "I feel like I need to be careful, because I know what bad things can happen. On the other, I know life is short and want to live it to the fullest. I kind of ride between those two polarities." You may be a driven risk taker, like Australian actor Guy Pierce, whose father was an air pilot tester whose plane crashed when Guy was eight. Or you may be at the other extreme, afraid of venturing into new challenges.

An interesting study of college students who'd had a parent die explored whether these young people perceived themselves as more vulnerable to death than their peers who had not experienced a parent's death. Not surprisingly, the answer was yes. The researchers concluded that this "perceived vulnerability" was a greater predictor of the possibility of adult anxiety and depression than the fact of the death of a parent. In other words, it's how the person *perceived* their vulnerability that mattered.[11] As we will see in the next chapter, anxiety has more to do with the stories we tell ourselves about what happens to us than the events themselves.

5. *Do You Generally Feel Lower Self-esteem Than You'd Like?*

"I am not against self-esteem, but I believe that self-esteem is just a meter that reads out the state of the system. It is not an end in itself. When you are doing well in school or work, when you are doing well with the people you love, when you are doing well in play, the meter will register high. When you are doing badly, it will register low. I have scoured the self-esteem literature looking for the causality as opposed to correlation, looking for any evidence that high self-esteem among youngsters *causes* better grades, more popularity, fewer teenage pregnancies, less dependence on welfare. There is nothing of this sort to be found in the literature. Self-esteem seems only to be a symptom, a correlate, of how well a person is doing in the world."[12]

I couldn't find anything in the literature that directly addressed a relationship between childhood parental bereavement and adult self-esteem, but if you've answered "yes" to this question, it's worth looking at further. My

belief is that self-esteem generates from what we tell ourselves about ourselves—the stories we create to make sense
of our world and our experiences. It's affected, of course,
by the messages others give us about who we are, but ultimately it's self-determined. As children, we are deeply
influenced by the opinions others have of us, and those
shape us in formative years. As adults, however, we don't
have to remain bound to what others have said about us
or done to us. We have choices about what we want to
think, believe, and feel. The literature of resiliency—the
ability to bounce back after tragedy—has some interesting
commentaries on the issue of self-esteem. In the study of
at-risk Hawaiian youth, which followed them from prebirth throughout their lives, the research showed several
predictors of positive self-evaluation at the age of thirty-
one or thirty-two. For men, the best predictor of positive
self-esteem was the number of sources of emotional support
they could draw on. For women, the best predictor of positive self-esteem was an internal locus of control.[13] This
leads to our sixth question:

6. Do You Believe That the Events of Your Life Are Mostly Random, Fate, Luck and Beyond Your Control?

This question hits at the heart of a key issue for children
and adults who've experienced traumatic losses—the issue

of control. When your parent died, you likely felt a strong sense of being out of control. You could not prevent your parent's death, and perhaps you believe in some way you contributed to it, by something you did or failed to do. We expect that our parents will be there for us throughout our lives, and losing a parent in childhood shatters that belief and upsets our sense of fairness. We feel literally out of control.

The Hawaiian resiliency study noted that resilient children, "by the time they were in high school, were significantly more likely than nonresilient children to have an 'inner locus of control'—a strong belief that they could control their fates by their own actions."[14]

One of the ways we address this issue in our work with children and teens at The Dougy Center is to help them regain their footing through exercising control over their choices. At the center, each group begins with a traditional "opening circle," which creates ritual and stability. Following the circle, each child decides what he or she would like to do during their unstructured time: play in the dress-up room, in the sand tray, art room, game room, stay and talk, go outside, or go to the volcano room, where they can safely hit and throw pillows and stuffed animals. Frequently they also select the adult facilitator or facilitators they want to accompany them. They direct their play, and we play along. We're not there as "experts" in their grief, telling them what they need to do to heal. We're there as students to learn from them because we believe that each grieving child is the expert in his or her own grief and needs. Through this process, they are empowered and regain a sense of control over their lives, even though they couldn't control the events of their parent's death.

Obviously there are many events in our lives, both positive and negative, that we can't control, and that seem random. But operating primarily from an external locus of control rather than an internal locus of control may contribute to a "victim" mentality. It can, literally, make you sick. This leads to the seventh question, which addresses not *what happens to you* but *the sense you make of what happens to you.*

7. Do You Feel Pessimistic and Hopeless About the Future?

I couldn't find any studies directly related to the issue of parental loss in childhood and adult attitudes toward life, though in my interviews, the majority of people said they believed ultimately they had been strengthened by this loss, and they approached the future with optimism. Many expressed how they'd transformed their loss into positive thoughts and actions. This gels with the findings of the Hawaiian resiliency study, which concluded that "a potent factor among high risk individuals who grew into successful adulthood was a faith that life made sense, that the odds could be overcome. They also had a more internal locus of control, a strong belief that they could control their fates by their own actions."[15]

When the originators of the "hopelessness theory" attempted to answer the question of why some people are resilient in the face of adversity and others are not, they found some crucial differences between the two groups. Those who were pessimistic globalized negative life events as the way the world is, assumed that negative consequences would follow, and believed something was fundamentally wrong with themselves for what happened. Optimists attributed negative life events to random situations, did not believe negative consequences had to follow, and did not believe these events meant that they were responsible or faulty in some way.[16]

Again, the literature supports that how we feel, and therefore how we act, is directly related to the internal messages we tell ourselves. If we envision a hopeless future, we will likely create one. It's not what happens to us that matters; it's what we do with what happens to us.

Now, let's look at what you can do to improve your life.

My Notes

_____

_____

_____

_____

_____

_____

_____

_____

_____

_____

_____

_____

_____

_____

_____

_____

_____

_____

_____

_____

_____

_____

What You Can Do Now to Address Your Parent's Death

Three Foundational Actions

In this chapter we're going to look at three actions you can take to address your parent's death, to aid your healing, and to improve your life. These are bold claims, I know. But I believe the three foundational actions discussed in this chapter are all necessary for optimal mental health. Practicing them doesn't mean it's "over," that you'll be happy all the time, or that you've resolved all your life issues forever. It will mean, however, that your life can take on a greater richness and meaning. In the next chapter, we will look at ten "activities" for you to consider that can help put you in touch with issues directly related to your parent's death. But first, this chapter provides the foundation for those activities.

Each of the three actions described here is necessary, like each leg in a three-legged stool. They're all interrelated, and of equal importance. The three foundational actions are:

1. Feel and express your emotions.
2. Share with others.
3. Exercise your power of choice.

Let's take a look at these one by one and see how they apply to your parent's death and your life now as an adult.

1. Feel and Express Your Emotions

My life was consumed with negativity. I couldn't express my love and compassion for people. Dealing with my father's death, even these long years later, has taken a wall down. I finally learned not to stifle or cover up who I am, that I can clearly face who I am, how I was formed, and embrace whatever the answer is. Only in coming to terms with myself, letting my feelings out, and letting them go, did I find access to becoming a productive, communicative human being.

—David, forty-three, whose father died when he was ten

The Role of Emotions

I believe most of us have a conflicted relationship with our emotions. We live in a culture that places emotions into categories of good and bad. Emotional well-being is often not taught or modeled by adults in elementary, middle, or high school, and we learn mostly by trial and error, and by watching and imitating others. Our culture judges when and how the expression of emotions is appropriate. For example, boys are encouraged not to cry, or they'll be seen as "wimps." Girls who express anger may be perceived as tough and unladylike. Although some slack is given to the grieving, boys continue to hear "You're the man of the house now," after the death of a father, and girls, especially the oldest, "You have to take good care of your dad and family now that your mother is gone." Not only do these directives put undue pressure on children to prematurely perform in adult roles, but they discourage the expression of emotions. They encourage us to keep our feelings inside.

We generally don't have as much difficulty with emotions that make us feel good, though I do know some people who seem unable to experience or express joy, happiness, or excitement. It's the other feelings, ones typically classified as "bad"—anger, fear, depression—we seem to have more trouble with. Often our method of handling these more painful emotions is to run from them, deny them, or try to anaesthetize ourselves from them through overworking, watching too much TV, compulsive shopping, eating, drinking, or staying busy.

But emotions are persistent little buggers. They don't go away until they've received the recognition they're after. They simply go underground. And they continue to try to get our attention, no matter how creatively we attempt to ignore them. My question for you is how are you handling your emotional being?

What Are Emotions For Anyway?

Emotions play many important roles in our well-being. They alert us when something is not quite right. They allow us to experience a full range of human existence, from exhilarating joy to crushing despair. I like to think of them as messages from our souls, trying to get our attention. When they fail to get our attention, they don't just pack up and leave.

Let's consider an example. Imagine you broke your leg, and you decided to ignore the pain and refuse treatment. It's possible that your bone would heal by itself, but chances are that even if it did, it wouldn't heal properly. If you continued to walk or run on it, you'd damage it further. Ignoring that your leg is broken does not change the fact that it's broken. It doesn't just go away because you're choosing to ignore it.

The same is true with emotions. Ignoring them doesn't

heal them. When we repress them, they remain bottled up inside us and eventually express themselves anyway, as symptoms.

The symptoms may be physical—headaches, sleeping difficulties, eating disorders, lower back pain, to name a few. They may be emotional—depression, feelings of inadequacy, worthlessness, or despair. They may be relational—fear of abandonment, inability to express love, sexual difficulties, clinging to people, or failing to allow others to get close.

As I interviewed adults who had a parent die in childhood, I found that they fell into three categories in how they described their history of relationships. Roughly a third said they were afraid to get close to anyone because "they might die, go away, or abandon me." A second group, also about a third, saw themselves as relentless "people pleasers," often compromising themselves in an effort to "hang on" to relationships, even when they weren't healthy. Only a third felt they'd achieved a healthy balance in their friendships and intimate relationships. Of course, the general population may show the same percentages, but it's something for you to consider: Which of the three groups do you fall into, and in what ways might your failure to feel and express your emotions play into it?

Another important question to look at is this: *Where do our emotions come from?* How you answer this question is very important because it determines whether you see yourself in the driver's seat of your life or whether you're in the backseat.

Sometimes emotions are automatic physiological responses. If someone walked in your room right now and pointed a gun at you, there's a strong chance you would experience fear. You'd also have thoughts that validated your fear: *I'm in danger. This is not good. I'm afraid. What can I do to stay alive?* What initially may be an automatic response receives additional support from what you tell yourself. I believe we underestimate how much our thoughts drive our emotions. Let me give you an example.

One evening, close to midnight, I was returning a rental car in downtown Portland. The office was closed, but a sign on the door instructed me to drop the keys in the slot. I did so before looking to see where my own car was parked. The lot was dark, I was alone, and I knew there was some potential danger in getting to my car, but I'd already returned the keys to the rental agency. I thought to myself, *This is exactly the kind of situation and setting where people get hurt,* and, all systems alert, I started to walk through the dark lot to find my car. Suddenly, a man jumped out from behind a truck and lunged at me. Because I was already aware of the potentially dangerous situation, I was able to run, screaming, down the street. My fear was at first reflexive, reactive, and probably a "built-in" self-preservation response. But even after I was safe, I continued to experience fear, though the incident itself was no longer a threat. My fear (and relief) came from what I was telling myself: *That was dangerous. I shouldn't have done that. I could have been killed. It's terrible that there are people in the world who want to hurt others.* All of those thoughts and feelings seem to be rational responses to the situation.

However, what if I told myself other stories: *It's never safe to be outside. Everyone in the world is out to get me.* What if my experience, and what I told myself about it, kept me in a place of fear?

The point I want to emphasize is that emotions are important markers, and they serve a healthy purpose, even the hard ones. They want to get our attention for very good reasons. When we classify some as "good" and some as "bad," we naturally want to avoid the "bad" ones, instead of befriending them. Instead of looking at them as bad, we would be better served to face them, embrace them, and ask them: *What are you trying to tell me? What can I learn from you?*

Some emotions are fleeting, and others seem to take up residence in our psyches. We all know people whose anger is bubbling just below the surface. We see people who seem to be controlled by anxiety or depression. What I'm suggesting is that emotions we refuse to face head on control us and keep us prisoners. It takes a tremendous amount of energy to hold emotions inside; energy that could be better spent! We try harder and harder to avoid them, without realizing we have the key to free ourselves. That key is choice.

After traumatic events, our bodies, minds, and emotions find ways to protect us. These necessary defenses allow us to survive and to go on. But sometimes these defenses don't go away. They act as night watchmen to keep us on the alert against further damage. Sometimes those responses become ingrained, automatic, even when they're no longer needed to protect us. We stay in ruts, letting our emotions control us instead of embracing them as welcome guests, listening to their stories, and deciding whether to invite them for a longer visit or show them the door.

Is it possible that you have emotional visitors who've stayed too long in the residence of your psyche? Do you ever feel controlled by your emotions, rather than the other way around? Perhaps you need to listen to their story. Then you can decide whether to invite them to hang around, change, or cordially escort them to the door.

I don't mean to say that embracing and expressing your emotions is a magical cure for all of your life issues. Remember, feeling and expressing your emotions is only one of the three legs of your psychological stool. But I believe that not embracing and not expressing emotions takes an enormous toll physically, psychologically, and relationally.

When I talk about feeling your feelings and expressing

your emotions, I'm not talking about rumination, the endless focus on something without change or movement. Let's consider rumination for a moment because there's considerable controversy within psychological circles about the role of emotional expression. At one end of the spectrum, there's the "no holds barred" expression—if you feel it, express it. At the other end is the belief that over-focusing on feelings and emotions feeds and perpetuates them, keeping people "stuck" in unhealthy patterns. I would say there's a healthy balance in-between: expressing emotions without hurting oneself or others, and finding therein both clarity and movement so that you're not held captive by them.

The word *rumination* originates from the Latin root *rumen,* meaning "throat." A secondary meaning of the word in contemporary American usage is "to chew cud, to reflect on over and over again." Chewing a cud is something that hoofed, horned mammals (called ruminants) do. These cattle, sheep, and goats collect food in the first of four divisions in their stomachs. This regurgitated, partially digested food (cud) is returned to their mouths for thorough chewing. In a literal sense, their nourishment is stuck in their throats! I'm not advocating rumination—endless regurgitated, partially digested emotional cud chewing. I'm talking about honestly embracing emotions, listening to them, expressing them, and choosing how much power you want to give them. I can't give you any time frames or schedules or norms about when feeling your feelings becomes rumination. I can only say that if you're happy where you are, stay where you are. If, on the other hand, you sense that you could be happier, more fulfilled, or more whatever words you'd use to describe the person you want to be, consider whether you have places of emotional stuckness.

I also do not want to suggest that *reckless* expression of emotions is curative. Continual, reckless, and indiscriminate expression usually makes things much worse. I'm not suggesting you should "let it all hang out" to anyone and everyone, damn the consequences. To express your emotions in times of vulnerability with those who aren't prepared to support you is counterproductive. This is best done within a therapeutic relationship or community, and may be with a friend, a relative, a support group, or a professional counselor.

There are several challenges here, especially if you're one of those people who has kept your emotions at a distance. One challenge is to allow yourself to open the door to feeling and experiencing what's possibly been locked up for a while. Another is to identify what's in there, what feelings you have. And a third is to find helpful, life-affirming ways to express your emotions. Those can be daunting challenges! You may be afraid to open that door because you don't know if you can handle what's inside. You may be concerned that you will not be able to handle your emotions, or that if you open the floodgates, they may never close. If this feels too daunting to face alone, I encourage you to find a counselor or therapist to assist you in your journey.

Why bother to express your emotions at all? This is a topic of great interest to psychologists and researchers in mental health concerns. One of the foremost researchers in this area is psychologist James Pennebaker, whose seminal book, *Opening Up: The Healing Power of Expressing Emotions,*[1] contains entertaining and powerful information on dozens of research studies illustrating how self-disclosure and the expression of emotions is good for both our emotional and physical health. From boosting our immune systems, through lowering blood pressure, and a host of other physical benefits, the studies clearly demonstrate the differences between those who disclose and those who do not. Other studies have also concluded that not disclosing painful or traumatic events can "aggravate the adverse health toll taken by such traumas."[2]

We saw earlier that children who had a parent die had a higher susceptibility for depression, anxiety, health problems, lower self-esteem, underperformance, external locus of control, and pessimism about the future. Although the research is inconclusive as to what degree these symptoms translate into adulthood, many of those I interviewed saw themselves in at least one of these categories, and some in all of them. I believe that how you handle your emotions—feeling them and expressing them—greatly influences your mental and physical health and how you view the world, something all of these "symptoms" touch on.

So before we move on to the second action, let's take a look at some common emotions following loss. See if you have glimpses of yourself. Remember that none of these emotions are "bad." They may become problematic if they're controlling you, rather than you controlling them. But each of them has a message; each of them wants to teach you something. We'll start with depression, since it appears to be one of the most common consequences of parental bereavement in childhood. Then we'll look at what to do with these emotions. First, they're asking to be heard, to be acknowledged, to be noticed.

Depression

I don't want to in any way minimize the crippling effects of chronic depression, depressive episodes, or manic depression. These are serious and life-threatening challenges. However, I believe we need to broaden our understanding of depression's causes and cures by understanding it as both a physical disease and a dis-ease of the spirit.

It's well-documented that there are biological components to depression; that is, the depressed person's brain chemistry and immunological systems are different from a nondepressed person's. In this sense, depression may be thought of as a physical disease, like leukemia, cancer, bronchitis, or diabetes. Depending on the severity of the disease, medication may be warranted, and, as in all diseases, habits and lifestyle choices help or hinder healing. Because depression changes body chemistry, sometimes medication to treat depression is warranted. As Frederic F. Flach, the author of *The Secret Strength of Depression* and *Resilience: The Power to Bounce Back When the Going Gets Tough,* notes; "For many patients, antidepressants accelerate the recovery from depression. I see them as resilience-enhancing drugs that act somehow, somewhere, to fill in a biochemical gap, and by putting the biological components of resilience in place again, allow the individual to call upon his own resilience to do the rest of the job."[3] Within this framework of understanding depression, some of us are more susceptible to inheriting depression, just as we may be at greater risk for breast cancer, blindness, alcoholism, and a host of other diseases and conditions based on family history and heredity.

But I also believe some forms of depression are not "diseases" that need to be controlled by medication, but "dis-ease" symptoms that can be mediated by changing how we think and act—by exercising the power of choice. This usually requires, or at least is enhanced by, therapy. If untreated, this type of depression begets a cycle of depression, which actually changes brain chemistry, influences mood, and alters how we look at the world. To what degree a specific individual's depression is physical and to what degree psychological can only be evaluated by a thorough medical and psychological examination. While medication may help restore equilibrium to a depressed person, there's also a down side to an overreliance on medicating. Drugs can prematurely mask our pain, decreasing our motivation to change what we have the ability to change in order to address our depression. If a diabetic person takes medication but continues to eat foods that foster the disease, the drugs may actually be counterproductive. Overdependence on drug cures for depression may increase our dependence on them, at least psychologically if not physically. I think it's noteworthy that despite all of our advances in understanding and treating depression, as well as the improvement in nonaddictive pharmaceuticals, we've seen the incidence of depression in the United States increase more than ten times over the last century.

Yet there is some "good news" about depression. The first good news is that it can ultimately be constructive. It can function as a warning bell that something is amiss and motivate you to address the situation. If we could envision depression as a message with meaning, rather than a terrible thing to be avoided at all costs, I believe we could better address underlying issues or contributing factors, rather than simply treat the symptoms and hope they'll go away. A wise therapist of mine, Dr. Linda Fritz, once told me that depression is "inspiration without form." After many years of suffering from depression, I'd always thought of it as something I wanted to get rid of. What I didn't realize was that I couldn't get rid of it by running, avoiding, or anaesthetizing myself. Linda's comment was the first time I'd ever thought of depression as something I could learn from, as a message from my soul. Depression alerts us that we need help.

The second piece of "good news" about depression is a bit tricky. Some who've studied depression extensively believe depressed people are actually more in touch with reality than those who are not depressed. There's a lot of supporting evidence, for example, that depressed people are more accurate judges of their skills than nondepressed people. Depressed people more accurately remember events, both good and bad, whereas those who are not depressed tend to inaccurately color events in a more positive light. "Realism," Martin Seligman proposes, "doesn't just coexist with depression, it is a risk factor for depression, just as smoking is a risk factor for lung cancer."[4] How could this possibly be "good news"? We'll discuss this aspect in more detail later in this chapter, but this reinforces that it's not what happens to us that determines the courses of our lives, but the meaning and the choices we make around these life events. It can actually give comfort to those who've suffered depression. Things may really be as bad as you think they are! You're not crazy!

Which leads to the third and perhaps most important "good news" about depression: With the assistance of a competent therapist, it can be treated successfully and the cycle broken. It's not that it's impossible to break the cycle without therapy, but like many patterns of behavior, it's hard for us to see ourselves objectively. Since the symptoms of depression include lower energy, hopelessness, and an inability to consider options that might help relieve the depression, it can become a self-fulfilling prophecy, fueling depression. We can literally become what our thoughts tell us we are. Medication may or may not be warranted to assist in restoring chemical balance and the energy to explore deeper issues, but I believe medication alone will ultimately only address the symptoms and not the roots of depression.

So if depression has shadowed you in your life, consider that this message from your soul may be trying to help you, to get your attention. Find a competent therapist and begin the journey out of depression and into full impact living!

Anxiety

Understandably, one of the common outcomes of early parental death is anxiety. Death at a young age alerts us to the reality that bad things happen, that we're not as safe as we thought we were, and that life can change dramatically in an instant. These are all true statements, with potentially anxiety-producing responses. The relevant issue for you now is to what degree, if any, you've carried that anxiety into your adult life. Again, remember that anxiety is not a "bad" emotion. It can alert you to real danger and protect you. It serves an important purpose. But if anxiety is an emotional lifestyle for you, if it controls the way you look at the world, rather than alerting you to specific occasions of potential danger, you may be expending precious energy that could be used in more constructive pursuits.

Anger

Anger is a logical response to something that doesn't seem fair, for example, that you were a child when your parent died. Why did your parent have to die? Why did this have to happen to you? Why not someone else? Your parents are supposed to be around to raise you, to pay for your food and clothing until you can work and fend for yourself. They're supposed to support and nourish you, and guide you through the problems and pitfalls of life. They're supposed to become grandparents to your children.

It didn't happen that way for you.

You have a "right" to feel angry.

When children are angry, something strange happens. Adults don't want them to be angry. They don't know how to validate appropriate anger and help children channel it constructively so that it doesn't hurt anyone. Many kids walk around like time bombs ready to explode; if adults

171

could help them find useful ways to express their anger, it would diffuse.

When your parent died, you may have felt anger toward him or her, especially if you believe his or her actions somehow contributed to your parent's demise, through suicide, for example, driving recklessly, smoking, or abusing drugs. You may have been angry at your parent simply for leaving you, even if he or she did nothing to contribute to his or her death.

You may also have been angry at your surviving parent. Why didn't he or she prevent this from happening? Or perhaps, why did this parent live and the other die?

Perhaps you were angry at God or fate. Sometimes people's belief systems interfere with the ability to admit or express anger. It may be viewed as a failure to trust God's sovereignty. If your belief system, whether Christian, Jewish, Muslim, Eastern or Western, included teaching that all events of life are part of God's will, you may have been discouraged from feeling or expressing anger. After all, who are you to question God?

You may also have been angry at yourself. Why didn't *you* prevent this? Maybe if you'd been a better son or daughter, if you'd worked harder, complained less, this wouldn't have happened.

You may have been mad at everyone and everything, surrounded by the unfairness of what happened to you, unable to escape the bell jar of anger.

And you may still carry some of that anger into your adult life. Is that possible?

Helplessness

As a child you were dependent on your parents for food, clothes, transportation, and other needs. Your "magical thinking," if you had a safe home environment, was that nothing bad would happen to you. Your parents would protect you. When your parent died, you were thrown into a different reality. You *were helpless* to prevent your parent's death.

That sense of helplessness as a child may have continued into your adulthood, generalizing into an overwhelming sense that you can't control anything that happens. Does this ring a bell for you? Do you find yourself overrelying on others to take care of or support you, at the expense of your own growth?

Guilt

Was there something you could have done to prevent your parent's death? Was there something you *wish you had done?*

As part of my doctoral dissertation on the effect of parental suicide on children, I asked kids between the ages of six and sixteen if they thought there was something they could have done to prevent their parent's suicide. Everyone had an answer, something they thought they could or should have done that may have prevented the death. Their responses ranged from the possible, through the improbable, to the impossible. "Maybe I could have saved my dad if I'd gone to live with him for the summer," said twelve-year-old Julie, whose parents were divorced. "I might have saved my father if I'd been a better daughter. He worried about me a lot," mused sixteen-year-old LaShanda. Fourteen-year-old Christopher expressed that "I should have found a way to prevent him from flying to Montana, like buying all the tickets on the plane so he couldn't go. If he hadn't gone there, he'd still be alive."

Believing you contributed to your parent's death in some way is not confined to those whose parent died by suicide. I've heard many children and teens say they thought something they did, or failed to do, in some way contributed to the death. One child took her mother's favorite scarf to school the day her mother was killed in a car accident. She was convinced that her act of disobedience directly caused her mother's death. A teenage boy believed his father's death from a heart attack was related to his failure as a son to be the athlete and scholar his father wanted.

So it's common for children to believe that their parent's death was related in some way to something they did or neglected to do.

Many kids also express guilt about other issues or events relating to their parent's death, like where they were or what they were doing at the time their parent died. A woman who was ten and at the movies when her father died expressed that she couldn't go to the movies for thirty years! A man who was at a theme park when his mother died forty years ago still expresses guilt at having a good time at the exact time his mother was killed. Not only does he have a continuing aversion to theme parks, parades, and carnivals, he finds it difficult to enjoy parties or gatherings where people are having fun.

Are you carrying a load of unresolved guilt?

Blame

We live in a time where it's become common to sue individuals and companies for their real or perceived contributions to mishaps, accidents, insults, or death. But blame is also a normal reaction to loss. Something unfair happened, and someone was at fault, or so the child's mind believes.

In some cases, there *is* someone to blame. If your parent was the victim of a drunk-driving crash, was murdered, or died as a result of someone's reckless behavior or inattention to safety, you have someone at whom to direct your feelings. Perhaps you can blame medical personnel—the doctor who didn't diagnose your parent's illness in time, the surgery that failed, the impersonal treatment your family received. You may blame your parent for his or her own

175

death. Perhaps he was diabetic and didn't take care of himself. Or your mother was driving recklessly. Another common culprit is God, especially if you were taught that God is a loving being who cares for all people. Perhaps your belief system was shaken, particularly if you had patronizing or superficial religious "pats on the back."

And, of course, you may blame yourself for your parent's death. If only you'd done something different, perhaps the result could have been different. Or perhaps on some deeper level, you believe your parent died because you were not a good enough son or daughter.

Has blame continued to haunt you in your adult life?

Relief

Ordinarily relief is thought of as a "positive" emotion, an easing of a burden or anxiety. We're relieved to find out we passed a test. Relieved a cancer scare is unfounded. But it's harder to express feeling relief when someone dies, except perhaps if they were suffering or in severe pain. Some kids I've worked with at The Dougy Center are afraid to express the ways in which they are relieved (or sometimes even glad) their parent died. "I know this isn't what I'm supposed to say," fifteen-year-old Miguel shared one night in group, "but I'm mostly glad my mom's dead. She was embarrassing, and she was really messing up my life. I'm actually relieved she's gone."

You may have felt relief that your parent died. Maybe your parent was abusive, absent, or drug addicted. I've tried to minimize my use of the phrase "death of a loved one" when speaking about death, because I've learned that some people cannot refer to their deceased parent this way. (Somehow the "death of a hated one" doesn't quite have a familiar ring, but it's closer to the truth for some kids.)

But you didn't have to be abused by your parent to experience relief. It may be that your parent was finally out of pain, either physically or emotionally. Perhaps you felt relief because you were out of the pain of seeing them in pain. Some who've had a parent with an extended illness die feel like their lives were on hold. After the death, they felt a new ability to return to life.

Numbness

Feeling numb or emotionally unresponsive is not unusual when a death occurs. Sometimes it takes awhile for the reality to sink in. There's a flurry of activity after the death that keeps everyone busy and occupied with tasks. In order to complete those responsibilities, we may need or choose to push our feelings away to make it through. Staying numb for a while may serve as a kind of emotional insulation, a way to protect our deepest selves. Forty-year-old Damien, reflecting on his father's death, says, "I think I had a massive shutdown after my father died when I was ten.

It was like, let's not mess with people or get to know them because you don't want the pain of whatever separation might come." He carried that numbness, that emotional shutdown, for nearly thirty years. Do you have patches and places of numbness that are waiting for your attention?

Once you've tapped into feelings that may have been buried, or are perhaps just bubbling below the surface, expressing them is the next challenge. If you have fear or concerns about how to do so, or how to do so safely, I highly recommend that you find a therapist or support group to assist you. If you have any kind of stigma associated with seeking help, notice this. It may be another way to keep yourself defended. Good therapists will not judge you or force you; they will assist you in your journey. I don't mean to suggest that you necessarily need professional help, but the second action for optimal mental health is to share with others. Let's take a look at this further.

2. Share with Others

There's a scene in the movie *The Prince of Tides,* based on Pat Conroy's novel, where the psychiatrist, played by Barbara Streisand, is counseling a man whose brother died, played by Nick Nolte. "All the talking in the world won't bring him back," Nolte's character tells the psychiatrist. "No," she replies. "But it might bring *you* back." If there are places where you might be *brought back,* I hope you will explore them.

When it comes to finding safe people to share your story with, my recent experience following the death of my father, and hundreds of stories I've heard, tell me there are three kinds of people: Those who don't want to listen; those who want to listen but it turns out can't; and those who want to listen and do.

Don't waste your time on trying to change people who clearly don't want to listen. Have compassion for those who want to listen but can't. They may have their own death-related issues that make it difficult for them to be there for you. They may not have well-developed listening skills and tend to want to fix things or try to make you feel better. What most grieving people say they want and need are people who will listen without judgment and without stepping in to tell them what to do unless asked. So this is probably not the time for you to try to educate others about listening. Reserve your emotional energy for those you know are willing and available to listen to you. If you can't find anyone, consider seeking out a qualified professional counselor or therapist. Paying someone to listen to you is better than stewing because you can't find anyone willing to hear your story. (For competent certified professionals in the death, dying, and bereavement field, you can contact the Association for Death Education and Counseling at www.adec.org.), or ask around through your local hospital or hospice. You might also consider attending a grief support group, though sadly, I'm not aware of any specifically for adults bereaved in childhood.

There are many examples of how sharing with others provides mental and physical health benefits. Consider just this one example: Over two hundred people participated in a study that surveyed their experiences of childhood trauma, including the death of a family member. They were also assessed for adult trauma and physical health. The findings revealed that those with the most health problems had suffered at least one childhood trauma that they had not confided to anyone. They had a higher incidence of cancer, high blood pressure, ulcers, flu, headaches, and earaches. It did not appear to be significant whether the trauma was a death in the family, sexual abuse, or physical abuse. The commonality was that the trauma had not been shared with others. The researchers concluded that "early childhood traumas that are not disclosed may be bad for your health as an adult."[5] It's not enough for you to just feel your emotions. We seem to have a built-in need to know that we've been heard, that we've been understood.

The third action for optimal mental health, the third leg of the stool, is perhaps the least understood of all three. Those who grasp its power, and who are willing to risk taking responsibility for their own lives, will be well on the path to living into their potential. I hope you will seriously consider practicing the power you have to make choices about your own life.

3. Exercise Your Power of Choice

Many of our problems stem from a fundamental belief that is not grounded in reality: that life should be fair. Consider just four representative facts out of thousands, which illustrate this point:

- Millions of children throughout the world do not have enough food to eat and will die as a result, even though there is enough food in the world to feed everyone.
- American prisons contain a disproportionate number of men of African heritage, while hundreds of European heritage males who commit "white collar" crimes walk free.
- Somewhere around 5 percent of American children will experience the death of a parent before the age of eighteen.
- Everyone on earth shares one common fate: We all will die. How fair is that?

Focusing on how life has let us down (the "life should be fair" syndrome) deters us from taking action to make positive change, paralyzing us from rolling up our sleeves and making the world a better place. I'm not saying we shouldn't feel bad, angry, mad, or sad about injustice or traumatic events. I'm saying we *should* feel what we feel, express it, share it, and not remain captive to anything that prevents us from being fully alive. I also believe the following five statements:

1. Life is not fair.
2. I am 100 percent responsible for how I feel.
3. I am responsible for the choices I have made in my life.
4. Although I can't control everything that happens to me, I can control how I choose to look at what happens to me.
5. I can choose to be positive and transform my experience into growth.

I believe that the death of a parent in your childhood was both a traumatic and potentially transforming event. And I believe that as an adult, you can transform that trauma, no matter what your current situation.

How? You can make the choice to do so. You can choose to be a victim or a victor. There's little doubt that you had some cards stacked against you. I'm not suggesting you weren't wounded or changed by your parent's death. But I also believe you developed some strengths that others who cruised through childhood without a trauma didn't develop. Can you identify what those strengths are? Perhaps you've developed a stronger compassion for others. You may have a deeper confidence that you can overcome obstacles, looking at what you've accomplished despite losing your parent. You may have a deeper commitment to family, knowing that life is fragile and unpredictable. Think for a moment about what you've learned and how you've grown as a person in spite of, or perhaps because of, your parent's absence from your life.

Choose to Be a Happy Person

Throughout many studies of the characteristics of happy adults, four characteristics emerge consistently.[6] They're not related to gender, social status, income, age, ethnicity, or life events. As you read these four characteristics, remember that as a parentally bereaved child, you were more likely than your nonbereaved peers to experience low self-esteem, an external rather than internal sense of control, and more pessimism about the future. Happy adults:

1. Report positive self-esteem.
2. Are optimistic about life.
3. Feel personal control.
4. Tend to be extroverts.

The good news is, happy people *choose* to be happy. I've come to believe it really is that simple. (Conversely, unhappy people *choose* to be unhappy.)

It's logical to ask which comes first; are people happy because they have these traits, or do these traits make people feel happy? The answer is probably a combination of the two. If you're an introvert, you may not want to or be able to become an extrovert. But you can *choose* to learn to feel good about yourself, to feel personal control, and to have an optimistic view toward life.

In another study of happiness, University of Illinois's Ed Diener and University of Pennsylvania's Martin Seligman compared twenty-two "very happy" college students (who scored in the top 10 percent on a variety of happiness measures) with sixty "average happy" and twenty-four "very unhappy" peers. The happiest students were more social, spent less time alone, and had strong relationships with family, friends, and partners.[7]

How do you learn to have positive self-esteem, to practice optimism, to feel personal control, to have strong relationships with biological or chosen family?

The same way you learn anything: practice, repetition, and reinforcement.

Take self-esteem. Where does self-esteem come from? I believe self-esteem is something we develop (or fail to develop) through childhood and into young adulthood by learning to accept and love ourselves with all of our strengths and weaknesses. We face significant challenges along the way, including family and friends who don't (and can't) meet all of our needs; magazines, TV, and other media telling us we're never thin enough, rich enough, smart enough, or good-looking enough; peer pressure to conform to standards set by other insecure adolescents, to name a few. As adults, however, we have more choice and power than I believe most of us take advantage of, regardless of how others view us. Ultimately self-esteem is just that: SELF-esteem. I believe self-esteem develops through a marriage of the person you want to be and the person you are. The bigger the discrepancy, the worse you feel about yourself.

What about optimism? What are the differences between pessimists and optimists? Can pessimists learn to be optimists? Yes, if they want to. And why wouldn't you want to? Perhaps fear of the unknown. Otherwise, why would so many people in the world choose to be unhappy? It's what they know. They're afraid to try to be happy lest they should fall on their face. Unfortunately, they also want to make others unhappy, to join their club. You know people like this, don't you?

Martin Seligman, author of *Learned Optimism: How to Change Your Mind & Your Life*[8] says that optimists view setbacks as temporary, changeable, and situation specific. Pessimists look at obstacles as permanent, unchangeable, and pervasive. Attitude does make a difference. It's what you tell yourself about what happens rather than what happens that determines outcome. University of Michigan psychologist Barbara Fredrickson's research on optimistic thinking styles reveals that how we think can be self-fulfilling.[9] We can create positive or negative outcomes based on how we view the world. The outcomes reinforce our view of the world, and we stay in the cycle of optimism or pessimism. We continue to blame others for the consequences of our own choices and decisions, without realizing the degree to which we have contributed to that outcome. (Don't you know someone who continues involvement with partners who disappoint them and let them down? Do they ask, "Why do I always wind up with losers?" Do they realize they are the only constant in the string of bad relationships?)

Why choose optimism over pessimism? Other than the fact that it's a more pleasant way to live, there are some health benefits as well. For example, pessimistic people are two to eight times more at risk of depression, according to Seligman.

If it seems overly simplistic to believe optimism is a choice, consider an example. Let's say you're in a relationship with someone you love and that person decides to end the relationship—an event that happens to most of us at some time in our lives. Here are some thoughts you could tell yourself:

- I'm a rotten person or he'd love me and want to be with me.
- She's a rotten person or she'd stay with me.

- No one will ever love me.
- I'll never be able to love anyone like I loved him.
- I can't stand the thought of her loving someone else.

None of these statements are facts; they are all interpretations of an event. You could also tell yourself these statements:

- I'm sorry things didn't work out, but I did what I could to make the relationship work.
- I can't control anyone else's feelings or actions, and though I wish we could stay together, it takes two to make that happen.
- I know I'm a loving person and that I can be in another fulfilling relationship if I decide to be.
- Neither of us were perfect. My challenge is to learn what I can so I can avoid making the same relationship mistakes over and over.
- Even though I feel hurt and sad at the ending of this relationship, his actions don't *make* me feel anything. I'm responsible for my own feelings and actions.

How do we choose to take control over our lives, to be optimistic, and to build self-esteem? Here are five ways. They really are simple, but they're also a conscious choice.

1. Recognize, accept, and believe that you have a choice and control over your life. Listen to your internal dialogue and the negative (or positive) messages you give yourself. Acknowledge that you can change those tapes!

2. Look outside of yourself. When we're depressed, we tend to become self-absorbed, to shut ourselves off from others, and to build a cycle of depression. Then we feel worse about ourselves, don't want to be around people, and (not surprisingly) they don't really want to be around us either. It can help to get involved in something that helps others, whether it's volunteering at a homeless shelter, with street kids, drug-affected babies, or the elderly. Sometimes we don't appreciate what we have until we lose it or until we put it into perspective. Focus on the strengths and blessings you *do* have, not what you don't have.

3. Smile—it's infectious. "Put on a happy face, and your body, either not knowing the difference or hoping for the best, responds as if the expression were genuine. The act of smiling engages at least three major muscle groups, increasing blood flow to the face and thus helping to create a rosy glow."[10] Ever notice how people who smile seem happier and friendlier than people who frown or scowl? It's because they are! Happiness is infectious, and unfortunately, so is negativity.

4. Laugh. Linda Richman, comedian Mike Myer's mother-in-law, faced many losses in her life, and wound up attending 103 self-help seminars looking for solutions and direction to overcome her pain. She distilled what she learned into the book *I'd Rather Laugh*.[11] The essence of her message? "Laughter is a choice. You have to make a decision that you want to have some joy in your life." The act of laughing even has some measurable health benefits; it increases antibody-producing cells and activates virus-fighting T cells in our immune systems.

5. As Winston Churchill said: "Never, never, never give up." This is your life. Are you living it to the fullest? It *is* your choice.

In the next chapter, we'll look at ten practical activities you can consider that may help you to further explore the effect of your parent's death on you now.

My Notes

Ten Practical Suggestions

*My father died when I was ten, but it wasn't until twenty years
later that I went to a counselor. I didn't go about my father, it was
about a relationship I was in. I realized how withdrawn I'd been,
how I couldn't create a committed relationship. I slowly started
getting my life straightened out. As this mystery started to be
unraveled, it was like the thread on your sweater: pretty soon the
whole sweater's gone. It has taken me years of different things—
counselors, friends, courses—to gain the perspective
that I lacked at the time.*

—David, thirty-five

As you read this chapter, please keep in mind that the
suggestions offered here are simply that: suggestions. You
may be in a place in your life where you don't need to do
anything to come to terms with your parent's death. If
you're content with what you've done and where you are,
that's okay. But if something here strikes a chord, give it
your consideration. You may be surprised at what you un-
cover and how it helps you. I believe we have an inborn
need to understand and make sense of things. When we

have unfinished business, it lurks in the background and wants to get out. What we don't know *can* hurt us! So, as you read the ten suggestions below, see what fits for you.

1. Get the Information You Need

Do you know everything you want to know about your parent's death and life? If not, it's not too late to find out. Sometimes the "not knowing" can keep us stuck. Some of the adults I've talked to are afraid to get the facts, unsure how to handle the information. To them I recommend enlisting a caring friend or family member to assist in the search. Of course, it's possible you don't want to know, and that's okay too; but if you do, there are multiple steps you can take. Consider one person's journey:

On April 19, 1945, four-year-old Ann Mix's father, Sydney Bennett, was killed in World War II. More than 406,000 men left an estimated 183,000 American children fatherless, often with little information about the circumstances of their deaths. At that time there was little encouragement to talk about emotions. Postwar fervor and "moving on" through victory absorbed the country, and survivors. In 1990, at the age of forty-nine, Ann began searching for WWII orphans in order to write about their experience and to gain understanding about her own. In 1991, she founded The American WWII Orphans Network, and in 1998 coauthored with Susan Johnson Hadler

Lost in Victory: Reflections of American War Orphans of World War II. The network has registered over three thousand people whose fathers died, as well as directing them to sources of information about their fathers from military and government records, war buddies, family, and friends. Their Web site, www.awon.org, includes a host of resources for World War II orphans, mostly in their fifties now, and has provided direction, solace, and information for thousands whose fathers died in the war.

Your parent may not have died in WWII, and you may have no interest in starting Web sites or writing books, but there are simple steps you can take to find out more about his or her life and death. Perhaps the most accessible step is to ask family members what they know or remember. I encourage you not to be afraid to ask for fear you will "dredge up" old memories and upset them. Most people are grateful that someone cares, and even if at first reluctant, will pour out their memories as if the events happened yesterday. If they don't want to, that's okay, but you'll never know unless you ask.

One June several years ago I called my mother to ask her about my sister, Lynne Cecilia, who'd died shortly after birth, my parent's first child. When she was born, my father was twenty, my mother nineteen. It had been forty-five years since her death, and I realized we'd never talked about her. I only knew about her at all because my grand-mother, in hushed tones, would attribute my mother's annual June blues to her probable reflections on the baby's death. When I called my mother, we spent several hours on the phone. She told me I was the first person who had ever asked about the baby or what it was like for her to be nineteen and lose her first child. For forty-five years, she'd kept her fears and feelings to herself. A couple years later we were talking about my parents' marriage, which had ended near their fortieth anniversary. "When did you realize it was over?" I asked her, and was startled by her response. She told me, her eyes tearing, "I think it started to end when I came home from the hospital without the baby, and we could never talk about it." I can barely imagine all of the ways that legacy affected their relationship, as well as me and my two brothers. In our phone conversation, my mother was able to release the pent-up feelings and share her experience, and the process itself was healing. An added benefit was a deepening of *our* relationship. Of course, I can't guarantee your experience will be as positive, but I again encourage you to not let fear or the desire to protect others prevent you from asking. You may be surprised at the healing that can take place, not just for you, but for others who are keeping secrets or have held feelings inside.

Another potential source of information about your parent's life and death is through their friends or associates. A fifty-five-year-old acquaintance of mine had very little information about her mother, who died giving birth to her. Shortly after the death, her father had remarried, and her stepmother demanded that all photos and belongings of her predecessor be destroyed. In her fifties, my acquaintance tracked down several friends of her mother's in England, some of whom were in their nineties, and was regaled with stories and photos of the mother she'd never seen.

In this age of sophisticated technology, there are multiple tools, including the Internet, useful in tracking people and information down. Several people I spoke with had enlisted private investigators to aid in their searches. You can obtain copies of death notices, obituaries, and, if relevant, police reports. Knowing more about your parent's life and death may help to bring comfort and a kind of closure to the unknown.

2. Continue a Connection with Your Parent

Contrary to popular belief, death does not end a relationship. While it ends the ability to connect on this physical flesh-and-blood plane, it doesn't preclude the possibility of ongoing connection. Our death-denying and death-averse culture encourages us to "get over it," "move on," "put it behind you," but in a very real way our lives are infused with the influence of others. Our cells, literally, carry our parent's memory. Why should we have to, or want to, close that door as if they no longer exist? Even if your belief system is that life ends at death, death does not end memories or dreams.

Children commonly and instinctively maintain connections with their deceased parent. They talk about it frequently in their groups at The Dougy Center. Phyllis Silverman and J. William Worden write about it in their respective books following their research in the Harvard Child Bereavement Study.[1] Silverman and Nickman discuss it more fully in a compelling chapter on how children "construct" their dead parent in the excellent book, *Continuing Bonds: New Understandings of Grief.*[2]

Here are two of the many ways children instinctively continue bonds. Perhaps you've experienced one or both of these. And perhaps it will help you, as an adult, to consider how you might continue to connect with your deceased parent.

Think of Your Parent Existing Somewhere

Almost 75 percent of the children in the Harvard Child Bereavement Study thought about their parent as existing somewhere. Some defined that "somewhere" as heaven; others in some other place where they imagined the parent living free of pain, happily enjoying a new phase of existence. Sometimes they imagine reuniting with their parent in that place. If your belief system includes that possibility, you may want to connect with your parent in that place, through your imagination, through writing, and through dreaming.

Connect with Your Parent Through Dreams and Symbols

Just over 80 percent of the Harvard study's children felt the experience of being watched, or watched over, by their deceased parent. I should mention that over half of them occasionally had some fear associated with this experience, usually because of the concern that their parent might disapprove of something they were doing. But many of them connected their deceased parent with a positive symbol— frequently a star, rainbow, or another aspect of nature.

It's not a practice confined to children. About a month ago my father was admitted to an intensive care unit in a Pennsylvania hospital. After nearly four weeks of ups and downs, the doctors told my stepmother Betty that his prospects were not optimistic, and that she might want to think about other options. He was not likely to come out of the coma, his lungs were not functioning, his heart was damaged, and essentially he was being kept alive by machines. As she agonized over what to do one Saturday morning on the back deck of the home they shared, a cardinal landed on the nearby railing, peered intently at her, and flew away. She and my father shared a love of birds, particularly cardinals, but joked about how only "blue" birds were frequenting the bird feeder of their new home. It was the first cardinal she'd seen, and she was convinced that it was "Charlie's angel," letting her know it was okay to let him go. She made the decision to let the doctors know on Monday that his suffering should end. The next morning, on Mother's Day, my father died. Betty believed, and I do too, that his parting gift was to die, sparing her from having to make that difficult decision. I will never see a cardinal the rest of my life without thinking of my father and the gift of his life and death. When he died, I bought a small ceramic cardinal for my kitchen windowsill, a symbolic reminder of my continuing connection to him.

I've talked with many children, teens and adults, who also maintain connection with a deceased parent through their dreams. Such dreams can be a source of healing, understanding and growth. I believe in a dream state, much like hypnosis, we may allow our judgmental and controlling "adult" selves to relax, and we connect with our deepest longings and fears. Dreams may be scary or safe, but they always have a messages for us, if we're willing to listen.

3. Create Rituals and Traditions for Remembering

Rituals are ceremonies that help us mark significant events. Most of us engage in rituals around major holidays, birthdays, and anniversaries. We also create traditions for those rituals. The word *tradition* comes from a Latin word meaning "to hand over, deliver, entrust." Some of our family traditions, as well as cultural traditions, are handed down from our families, and others are ones we create ourselves.

When it comes to traditions around death, the main-stream American culture has some work to do. Although the funeral industry has come a long way, there's a lot more that could be done to incorporate children into the whole process.[3] In the days and sometimes weeks after a death, there are cards and flowers and tuna casseroles from friends, and then: nothing. When it comes to after-death acknow-ledgment, rituals, and traditions, we're pretty much on our own.

Some cultures have traditions like Mexico's Day of the Dead fiesta, where the memories of deceased relatives are invoked through rituals such as placing their names on cakes and candies in the shapes of skulls and coffins. "This practice assures the spirits of the dead that they have not been forgotten by the living and provides solace to the living in the form of tangible symbols of the presence of deceased loved ones."[4] In Judaism, there is the practice of Shivah, a formal mourning period, with the reciting of the Kaddish, the Jewish prayer for the dead. During the year following a death, it is recited by mourners and then on the anniversary. These rituals help honor and remember the deceased in formal ways.

Many of us don't have cultural or religious traditions to help us remember our parent's life and mark his or her death, so we have to invent them. The options really are unlimited. The biggest hurdle may not be what to, but giving yourself permission to do something. Here are some suggestions for your consideration, and I'd encourage you to create your own:

- If you missed your parent's funeral or memorial (or if none was held, or if the one that was held holds bad memories for you), you can hold your own memorial service, alone, with friends or family.
- Make (or buy) cards on Mother's Day or Father's Day, as well as their birthday. Write on it what you'd like to say now or what you wished you'd had a chance to say. Celebrate the times you had with them. This Father's Day will be the first one since my father died. It's been hard to see cards and ads in the paper for this celebration. I decided that I would select a card anyway, write what I wished to say to him, and share it with my stepmother.
- Visit their burial site or a place they loved, knowing that death does not have to mean a final good-bye. Talk to them and let them know what's happening in your life now, celebrating their life on their birthday,
- Hang photos (and don't be afraid to talk to them).
- Have a ceremony of some kind to mark the event. The evening of Father's Day I lit a candle with a friend as we shared memories, tears, and laughter.

4. Write It Out

Give sorrow words; the grief that does not speak
Whispers the o'er fraught heart and bids it break.

—William Shakespeare

Research has shown that certain kinds of writing can have a positive effect on mental health, particularly expressive writing and journaling. In one study, fifty students wrote for twenty minutes a day four days in a row. Half were assigned to write about their thoughts and feelings related to a trauma they had experienced. These students disclosed incidences of rape, abuse, suicide attempts, deaths, and other losses. The other twenty-five students were told to write about superficial topics. All of the students agreed to have their blood drawn and tested three times: the day before the writing assignments began, after the last writing session, and six weeks later.

Lab researchers analyzed the blood samples by measuring the white cells that control immune function. These antibodies can slow down or destroy bacteria and viruses. Their findings? "People who wrote about their deepest thoughts and feelings surrounding traumatic experiences evidenced heightened immune function compared with those who wrote about superficial topics."[5] This result persisted in the six-week follow-up. Additionally, those who wrote about traumas had a drop in health center visits compared to those who wrote about other topics.

Other studies have found that writing that includes a description of your experience, the feelings associated with the experience, and reflections on how you feel about it have the most benefit. Just describing the experience or just writing about the feelings was not found to be as therapeutic as including the meaning or sense you make of what happened.[6] There's evidence that it's not just the expression that's curative, it's also about feeling and understanding you're not alone. So you may wish to share your writing with a trusted friend or relative, in a support group, or with a therapist. Try writing a letter to your parent. You don't have to know what to say before you start—just dig in. You may be surprised by what comes out. For journaling, here are some sample questions to get you started:

- When did your parent die?
- How old were you at the time?
- What do you remember being told about the death? (Where you were, who told you, what they said.)
- If you were of school age, what was it like going back?
- Who was helpful and in what ways?
- Were there ways people were not helpful?
- If you went to the funeral or service, what do you

remember about that? Were there things you would have liked to be different?

- If you didn't attend a funeral or service, how do you feel about that now?
- In what ways did your life change after your parent's death?
- Who in your family do you think was most affected and how?
- In what ways did your parent's death strengthen you, if any?
- How do you think your parent's death has affected your relationships?
- In what ways do you imagine yourself more challenged than kids who didn't have a parent die?
- If you could give advice to adults who have a parentally bereaved child the age you were when your parent died, what would you say?
- What might you say to a child whose parent died at the same age you were when your parent died?
- How old would your parent be now if he or she had lived? What would you imagine your relationship would likely be?
- What meaning do you make now of the reasons for your parent's death?

Don't straitjacket yourself by trying to write the perfect tome. On the other hand, many bereaved people have successfully written articles and books that have helped count-less others as they shared their experience. Is there a book or article in you?

5. Expressive Arts

Yes, Shakepeare said to "give sorrow words," but then again, he was a writer. William Wordsworth, another writer, was said to be so distraught after his brother's ac-cidental drowning that he stopped talking for four months. When he wrote again, he wrote this line: "A deep distress hath humanized my soul."

So giving sorrow words is great. But we should also consider giving sorrow paint and clay and markers and long walks and punching bags and music and dance and crayons. You might try expressive arts through taking a class or just rolling up your sleeves and doing your own thing. Finger paint. Trance dance. Color. Make a drawing of your family before and after the death. Get some clay and see what your hands form with it. Not all thoughts and feelings can be expressed in words.

6. Make Memory Book, Box, Container, Table, or—?

Never underestimate the power of of symbolic objects, in-cluding photographs. At The Dougy Center we have a closing ceremony for the children and adolescents that was developed by the center's founder, Beverly Chappell, an avid rock hound. Children who are closing from their group select three polished rocks, which have been through a lengthy and tumultuous tumbling process. These beautiful rocks symbolize the healing that has taken place for them during their sharing and participation at the center. They also receive a rough, unpolished rock with sharp edges and a duller exterior. The fourth rock represents the part of them that's still in progress and always will be since there is no "Grief Finish Line." All four rocks are passed around the circle of child participants and adult facilitators, as they share a memory with, make a wish for, or tell a story to the one who's closing from the group. The rocks are placed in a small, soft pouch with a drawstring and given as a parting gift. Many of the kids tell us they plan to put it with other possessions they have that belonged to their parent.

If you don't have a memory box or book, consider making one. The box can hold items that belonged to your parent or items you collect now that bring back memories. They can include photos as well. You can create a memory bulletin board. You could buy an unfinished table and paint it with memories or paste photos on it and shellac it. Make a memorial platter or ceramic piece at one of the many do-it-yourself stores. Do a collage with clippings from magazines. The possibilities truly are endless.

If you'd like to write a journal, you can make your

own or purchase one. Check out Compassion Books at www.compassionbooks.com or Centering Corporation at www.centering.org for options. The journal may include letters, photos, cards, and your own writings. Engaging in this kind of memory making may be very healing for you.

7. Make Something Good Happen.

I've placed a lot of emphasis on the power of expression through expressing feelings because I believe that restraining emotion takes a toll on one's emotional and physical health. But everyone has different levels of intensity and emotional makeup, and for some people rolling up their sleeves and doing something active is the channel they need.

- In your parent's memory, raise money for an organization that helps people (Mothers Against Drunk Driving, diabetes, cancer).
- Start an organization.
- Start an endowment fund through a local community foundation or organization in your parent's name.
- Start a support group.
- Make a Web site.
- Write a book.

Many of the nonprofit organizations in the United States have been started because of the experience of one family. Is there any way that you can commemorate your parent's life, transform their death, and help the world, even if it's just one person at a time?

8. Help Others: Volunteer

There's something very therapeutic about volunteering. When you're in the right volunteer job, you know you're getting more from it than you're giving. It can be healing in and of itself, particularly if you're doing something you have a personal investment in. If your parent died of cancer, leukemia, MS, or other disease, consider calling your local chapter or society and asking how you might help. If your parent was murdered or suicided, there are many excellent organizations working for prevention and assistance. Most nonprofit organizations can use help in office and yard work, events, fund-raising, board development, and would be happy to find a way for you to volunteer.

9. Take Care of Yourself

The process of grieving, even if it's many years after the loss, can be draining, emotionally and physically. During and after acute stress, our immune systems are weakened, more vulnerable to viruses, colds, and bacteria. It's important to make a conscious effort to take care of yourself. You know the usual suggestions: eat well, drink plenty of water, and get at least three weekly sessions of thirty minutes each in some kind of exercise—walking, swimming, biking, or a sport you enjoy.

But there's more you can do, or rather not do. Give yourself a break and relax! Relaxation can support strengthening of the immune system. The founder of the Mind/Body Medical Institute at Harvard Medical School, Herbert Benson, suggests a variety of techniques that contribute to less muscle tension, a lower heart rate, more efficient use of oxygen, and an increase in slower brain waves, known as alpha waves. These include meditation, yoga, and the practice of prayer. Other studies have demonstrated the positive effect of relaxation on chronic pain, diabetes, upper respiratory infections, asthma, and other illnesses.

In a survey of people who had a spouse die by suicide or in car accidents, the more people prayed about the deceased, the healthier they were. In fact, they were as healthy as the people who talked to friends or family about the death. James Pennebaker comments that "it is easy to see why this is true: Prayer is a form of disclosure or confiding." [7]

10. Find Meaning in Your Story

Ultimately, I believe one of the most important things you can do in coming to terms with your parent's death and how it has affected your life is transforming this loss into meaning with optimism and hope. What do I mean by finding meaning? Almost every child or adult who has a death asks, *Why did this happen to me?* In exploring and finding your own answers, I hope you will appreciate the person you are today and what you've overcome to be who you are and where you are.

I welcome your comments and suggestions:

> Donna Schuurman
> The Dougy Center
> P.O. Box 86852
> Portland, OR 97286
>
> donna@dougy.org

My Notes

Appendix
Limitations of Studies:
How To Know What to Believe When You Read a Study's Findings

A lot of conclusions are drawn from studies as if they are true, but to really know how to interpret and evaluate findings, you have to weigh many factors. We'll never have the 100 percent perfect, infallible study of bereaved children because we would have to literally study them before birth and into death with a very large population, which would be both costly and impractical. But like bad breath is better than no breath, imperfect studies are better than no studies at all. The key is assessing how to evaluate them and having a critical eye for generalizations that should not be made based on the limitations of the study. Here are a dozen common limitations:

1. *Studies of only one child.* Studying one bereaved child may be an interesting case study, but you can't make assumptions about all bereaved children because of one child's experience.

2. *No control group.* As interesting as it is to study a group of bereaved children, unless you also compare them to a group of their nonbereaved peers, matched by as many commonalities as you can, you can't assume that what you observe in the bereaved children is because they're bereaved.

3. *Small sample studies.* When the sample size is small, it reduces the ability to see differences between groups, or to know if they are significant when differences appear. So even if you have a control group, if you only have five kids in each group, it doesn't provide a large enough sample to show anything.

4. *Studies at one moment in time.* Studies that reflect bereaved children's experiences at one moment in time, for example a year after the death, may give us helpful, though limited information. These "nonlongitudinal," that is, not following children over time, studies don't help us understand how and what changes as children get older.

5. *Self-reporting.* Credible researchers are understandably wary of the accuracy of self-report. At The Dougy Center, we often find that what the child says about how he or she is coping is completely different from what the parent says. Both reports are subjective and can't be scientifically validated.

6. *Describing the population.* Many interesting studies have described the population of bereaved children, but descriptions don't equal cause. A lot of parents at The Dougy Center ask whether their child is acting the way he's acting because his father died or whether it's because he's a teenager. My response is: Who knows? Either way, if the behavior is of concern, it needs to be addressed. I don't think we can ever fully comb out these knotted behaviors and view them as single strands.

7. *Using special populations.* Studies have been conducted (usually without control groups) around special populations of bereaved children, for example, children in support groups, in residential treatment facilities, hospitals, New York City, etc. Whatever findings occur in a specialized population cannot be generalized to other populations.

8. *Retrospective studies.* One of the most common type of study is the retrospective, that is, asking groups of adults—bereaved as children—to reflect back on their experience. In addition to the complication of self-report, retrospective studies can never imply cause. That is, although you may feel that your father's death and your fear of attachment contributed to your seven divorces, it can't be scientifically proven.

9. *After-the-fact studies.* This is a complication of all studies of human subjects: since we can't accurately predict which children will have a parent die until the parent is diagnosed with a limited life span or actually dies, most studies are by necessity after the fact. If we look at a group of bereaved children, we can't compare them to what they were like before the death occurred, so we don't have quality measures to look at individual (or group) change.

10. *Questionable measurement tools.* As fun as it is to develop a questionnaire, valid measurement tools go through rigorous testing for internal and external validity and reliability, which is *definitely* outside the scope of this discussion. If you're really interested, check out a statistics book. Suffice it to say that the quiz someone developed for their dissertation, though it may shed light on the topic, isn't likely to scientifically show us much.

11. *Controlling for differences in time since the death.* In most studies the time since the death occurred is neither controlled for nor reported. This doesn't allow us to see if there are differences in bereavement based on length of time since the death. For example, it may be that kids seem to be doing well six months later, but in two years they fall apart. We can't gather information about this if we don't know the time since death in a specific study or if we don't factor that into our findings.

12. *Using just one data-collection method.* Valid studies don't just use one testing instrument. It's better to test the child, the parent, and perhaps others involved in the child's life. It costs more and takes more time, but provides more validity to whatever assumptions may be drawn from the data.

Notes

CHAPTER ONE: Feelings: Forget the Stages

1. E. Kubler-Ross, *On Death and Dying* (New York: Macmillan, 1969).

2. J. Bowlby, *Attachment and Loss, vol. 3, Loss, Sadness, and Depression* (New York: Basic Books, 1980).

3. J. W. Worden,*Grief Counseling and Grief Therapy: A Handbook for the Mental Health Practitioner*, 2nd ed. (New York: Springer, 1991).

CHAPTER TWO: Was I a Normal Grieving Kid

1. W. Middleton, B. Raphael, N. Martinek, and V. Misso, "Pathological Grief Reactions," in Eds. *Handbook of Bereavement: Theory, Research and Intervention*, M. Stroebe, W. Stroebe, and R. O. Hansson (New York: Cambridge University Press, 1993), pp. 44–61.

2. J. R. Lutzke, T. S. Ayers, I. N. Sandler, and A. Barr, "Risks and Interventions for the Parentally Bereaved Child," in *Handbook of Children's Coping: Linking Theory and Intervention*, eds. Wolchik and I. Sandler (New York: Plenum Press, 1997).

CHAPTER THREE: I Didn't Just Lose My Parent . . .

1. J. W. Worden, *Children and Grief: When a Parent Dies* (New York: Guilford Press, 1996).

2. E. Shneidman, *The Suicidal Mind* (Oxford: Oxford University Press, 1996).

3. E. Shneidman, *Suicide as Psychache* (Northvale, N.J.: Jason Aronson, 1993).

CHAPTER FOUR: How Others Influenced Your Grieving

1. V. Satir, *Peoplemaking* (Palo Alto Science and Behavior Books, 1972).

2. J. W. Worden, *Children and Grief: When a Parent Dies* (New York: Guilford Press, 1996).

3. J. Hollis, *The Middle Passage: From Misery to Meaning in Midlife* (Toronto: Inner City Books, 1993).

4. J. Hollis, p. 13.

CHAPTER SIX: What We Know About Children and Resiliency: The Good, the Bad, and the Ugly

1. E. E. Werner and R. S. Smith, *Overcoming the Odds: High-Risk Children from Birth to Adulthood* (New York: Cornell University Press, 1992).

2. N. Garmezy, "Resilience in Children's Adaptation to Negative Life Events and Stressed Environments," *Pediatric Annals* 20, no. 9 (1991), pp. 459–66.

3. Smith, and Werner, p. 177.

4. K. Butler, "The Anatomy of Resilience," *Family Therapy Networker* (March/April, 1997), p. 27.

5. Butler, p. 25.

6. The ten factors (but not the statements) are from H. I. McCubbin, M. A. McCubbin, A. I. Thompson, S. Han,

and C. T. Allen, "Families Under Stress: What Makes Them Resilient," *Journal of Family and Consumer Sciences* (Fall 1997), pp. 2–11.

7. Butler, p. 24.

8. S. J. Wolin, and W. S. Wolin, *The Resilient Self: How Survivors of Troubled Families Rise Above Adversity* (New York: Villard, 1993).

9. Wolin and Wolin, p. 113.

10. D. Black, "Sundered Families: The Effect of Loss of a Parent," *Adoption and Fostering* 8 (1984), pp. 38–43.

11. Black, p. 41.

12. R. S. Pynoos, "Grief and Trauma in Children and Adolescents," *Bereavement* Care 11 (1992), pp. 2–10.

13. Pynoos, p. 9.

14. M. J. Horowitz, C. Marmar, D. S. Weiss, K. DeWitt, and R. Rosenbaum, "Brief Psychotherapy of Bereavement Reactions," *Archives of General Psychiatry* 41 (1984), pp. 438–48.

15. Horowitz et al., p. 443.

CHAPTER SEVEN: How Your Parent's Death in Childhood Affects You Now

1. William Styron, *Darkness Visible: A Memoir of Madness* (New York: Random House, 1990).

2. C. Lloyd, "Life Events and Depressive Disorder Reviewed: Events as Predisposing Factors," *Arch General Psychiatry* 37 (1980), pp. 529–35.

3. T. Crook and J. Elliot, "Parental Death During Childhood and Adult Depression: A Critical Review of the Literature," *Psychological Bulletin* 87 (1980), pp. 252–59.

4. G. Barnes and H. Prosen, "Parental Death and Depression," *Journal of Abnormal Psychology* 94 (1985), pp. 64–69.

5. D. Zall, "The Long-Term Effects of Childhood Bereavement: Impact, on Roles as Mothers." *Omega Journal of Death and Dying* 29 (1994), pp. 219–30.

6. K. Adam, A. Bouckoms, and D. Streiner, "Parental Loss and Family Stability in Attempted Suicide," *Archives of General Psychiatry* 39 (1982), pp. 181–85.

7. T. Hallstrom, "The Relationship of Childhood Socio-Economic Factors and Early Parental Loss to Major Depression in Adult Life," *Acta Psychiatrica Scandinavica* 75 (1987), pp. 212–16.

8. *Newsweek* (June 14, 1999).

9. Zall.

10. Hallstrom.

11. G. C. Mireault and L. A. Bond, "Parental Death in Childhood: Perceived Vulnerability, and Adult Depression and Anxiety," *American Journal of Orthopsychiatry* 62 (1992), pp. 517–24.

12. M. E. Seligman, *Learned Optimism* (New York: Simon & Schuster, 1998), pp. vi, vii.

13. Werner.

14. Butler, p. 27.

15. Werner, p. 177.

16. L. Y. Abramson, G. I. Metalsky, and L. B. Alloy, "Hopelessness Depression: A Theory-Based Subtype of Depression," *Psychological Review* 96 (1989), pp. 358–72.

CHAPTER EIGHT: What You Can Do Now to Address Your Parent's Death

1. J. Pennebaker, *Opening Up: The Healing Power of Expressing Emotions* (New York: Guilford Press, 1990).

2. K. Petrie, R. Booth, and K. Davison, "Repression, Disclosure, and Immune Function: Recent Findings and Methodological Issues," in *Emotion, Disclosure, and Health,* J. Pennebaker, ed. (Washington, D.C.: American Psychological Association, 1995), p. 224.

3. Frederic F. Flach, *Resilience: The Power to Bounce Back When the Going Gets Tough* (New York: Hatherleigh Press, 1997), p. 109.

4. M. Seligman, *What You Can Change . . . and What You Can't* (New York: Fawcett Columbine, 1993), p. 199.

5. Pennebaker, pp. 19, 20.

6. D. Myers, "Hope and Happiness," in *The Science of Optimism and Hope,* J. Gillman, ed. (Philadelphia: Templeton Foundation Press, 2000), p. 329.

7. E. Diener and M. Seligman, "Very Happy People," *Psychological Science* (January 2000), pp. 81–85.

8. M. Seligman, *Learned Optimism: How to Change Your Mind and Your Life* (New York: Pocket Books, 1998).

9. B. Fredrickson, "Rewarding Positive Psychology," *Family Therapy Networker* (September/October 2000), p. 20.

10. V. Monroe, "When You're Smiling," *O* (May 2001), p. 184.

11. L. Richman, *I'd Rather Laugh: How to Be Happy Even When Life Has Other Plans for You* (New York: Warner Books, 2001).

CHAPTER NINE: Ten Practical Suggestions

1. P. Silverman, *Never Too Young to Know: Death in Children's Lives* (New York: Oxford Press, 2001).

2. P. R. Silverman and S. L. Nickman, "Children's Construction of Their Dead Parent," In *Continuing Bonds: New Understandings of Grief*, D. Klass, P. R. Silverman, and S. L Nickman, eds. (Washington, D.C.: Taylor & Francis, 1996), pp. 73–86.

3. The Dougy Center, *What About the Kids? Understanding Their Needs in Funeral Planning and Services* (Portland, Oreg: The Dougy Center, 1999).

4. L. A. DeSpelder and A. L. Strickland, *The Last Dance: Encountering Death and Dying* (Boston: McGraw Hill, 2002), p. 67.

5. J. Pennebaker, *Opening Up: The Healing Power of Expressing Emotions* (New York: Guildford Press 1997), p. 36, 37.

6. L. DeSalvo, *Writing as a Way of Healing: How Telling Our Stories Transforms Our Lives* (San Francisco: Harper, 1999), pp. 25, 26.

7. Pennebaker, p. 24.

References

Abramson, L. Y., G. I. Metalsky, and L. B. Alloy. "Hopelessness Depression: A Theory-Based Subtype of Depression." *Psychological Review* (1989).

Adam, K., A. Bouckoms, and D. Streiner. "Parental Loss and Family Stability in Attempted Suicide." *Archives of General Psychiatry* (1982).

Barnes, G., and H. Prosen. "Parental Death and Depression." *Journal of Abnormal Psychology* (1985).

Black, D. "Sundered Families: The Effect of Loss of a Parent." *Adoption and Fostering* (1984).

Bowlby, J. *Attachment and Loss, vol. 3, Loss, Sadness, and Depression.* New York: Basic Books (1980).

Butler, K. "The Anatomy of Resilience." *Family Therapy Networker* (March/April 1997), p. 27.

Crook, T. and J. Elliot. "Parental Death During Childhood and Adult Depression: A Critical Review of the Literature." *Psychological Bulletin* (1980).

DeSalvo, L. *Writing as a Way of Healing: How Telling Our Stories Transforms Our Lives.* San Francisco Harper, 1999.

DeSpelder, L. A. and A. L. Strickland. *The Last Dance: Encountering Death and Dying.* Boston: McGraw Hill, 2002.

Diener, E., and M. Seligman. "Very Happy People." *Psychological Science* (January 2002), pp. 81–84.

The Dougy Center. *What About the Kids? Understanding Their Needs in Funeral Planning and Services.* Portland, Oreg.: The Dougy Center, 1999.

Flach, F. *Resilience: The Power to Bounce Back When the Going Gets Tough.* New York: Hatherleigh Press, 1997.

Fredrickson, B. "Rewarding Positive Psychology." *Family Therapy Networker* (September/October 2000).

Garmezy, N. "Resilience in Children's Adaptation to Negative Life Events and Stressed Environments." *Pediatric Annals* 20, no. 9 (1991), pp. 459–66.

Hallstrom, T. "The Relationship of Childhood Socio-Economic Factors and Early Parental Loss to Major Depression in Adult Life." *Acta Psychiatrica Scandinavica* (1987).

Hollis, J. *The Middle Passage: From Misery to Meaning in Midlife.* Toronto: Inner City Books, 1993.

Horowitz, M. J., C. Marmar, D. S. Weiss, K. DeWitt, and R. Rosenbaum. "Brief Psychotherapy of Bereavement Reactions." *Archives of General Psychiatry* 41 (1984), pp. 438–48.

Kubler-Ross, E. *On Death and Dying.* New York: Macmillan, 1969.

Lloyd, C. "Life Events and Depressive Disorder Reviewed: Events as Predisposing Factors." *Arch General Psychiatry* (1980).

Lutzke, J. R., T. S. Ayers, I. N. Sandler, and A. Barr. "Risks and Interventions for the Parentally Bereaved Child." In *Handbook of Children's Coping: Linking Theory and Intervention.* Edited by Wolchik and I. N. Sandler. New York: Plenum Press, 1997.

McCubbin, H. I., M. A. McCubbin, A. I. Thompson, S. Han, and C. T. Allen. "Families Under Stress: What Makes Them Resilient." *Journal of Family and Consumer Sciences* (1997).

Middleton, W., B. Raphael, N. Martinek, and V. Misso. "Pathological Grief Reactions." In *Handbook of Bereavement: Theory, Research and Intervention.* Edited by M. Stroebe, W. Stroebe, and R. O. Hansson. New York: Cambridge University Press, 1993.

Mireault, G. C., and L. A. Bond. "Parental Death in Childhood: Perceived Vulnerability, and Adult Depression and Anxiety." *American Journal of Orthopsychiatry* (1992).

Monroe, V. "When You're Smiling." *O* (May 2001): p. 184.

Myers, D. "Hope and Happiness." In *The Science of Optimism and Hope.* Edited by J. Gilman. Philadelphia: Templeton Foundation Press, 2000.

Pennebaker, J. *Opening Up: The Healing Power of Expressing Emotions.* New York: Guilford Press, 1997.

Petrie, K., R. Booth, and K. Davison. "Repression, Disclosure, and Immune Function: Recent Findings and Methodological Issues." In *Emotion, Disclosure and Health.* Edited by J. Pennebaker. Washington, D.C.: American Psychological Association, 1995.

Pynoos, R. S. "Grief and Trauma in Children and Adolescents." *Bereavement Care* (1992).

Richman, L. *I'd Rather Laugh: How to Be Happy Even When Life Has Other Plans for You.* New York: Warner Books, 2001.

Satir, V. *Peoplemaking.* Palo Alto: Science and Behavior Books, 1972.

Seligman, M. *Learned Optimism: How to Change Your Mind and Your Life*. New York: Simon & Schuster, 1998.

Seligman, M. *What You Can Change . . . and What You Can't*. New York: Fawcett Columbine, 1993.

Shneidman, E. *The Suicidal Mind*. Oxford: Oxford University Press, 1996.

———. *Suicide as Psychache*. Northvale, N.J.: Jason Aronson, 1993.

Silverman, P. *Never Too Young to Know: Death in Children's Lives*. New York: Oxford Press, 2000.

Silverman, P. R., and S. L. Nickman. "Children's Construction of Their Dead Parent." In *Continuing Bonds: New Understandings of Grief*. Edited by D. Klass, P. R. Silverman, and S. L. Nickman. Washington, D.C.: Taylor & Francis, 1996.

Styron, W., *Darkness Visible: A Memoir of Madness*. New York: Random House, 1990.

Werner, E. E., and R. S. Smith. *Overcoming the Odds: High Risk Children from Birth to Adulthood*. New York: Cornell University Press, 1992.

Wolin, S. J., and W. S. Wolin. *The Resilient Self: How Survivors of Troubled Families Rise Above Adversity*. New York: Villard, 1993.

Worden, J. W. *Children and Grief: When a Parent Dies*. New York: The Guilford Press, 1996.

Worden, J. W. *Grief Counseling and Grief Therapy: A Handbook for the Mental Health Practitioner*. 2nd ed. New York: Springer, 1991.

Zall, D. "The Long-Term Effects of Childhood Bereavement: Impact, on Roles as Mothers." *Omega Journal of Death and Dying* (1994).